File... Don't Pile!™
A Proven Filing System for Personal and Professional Use

By

Pat Dorff

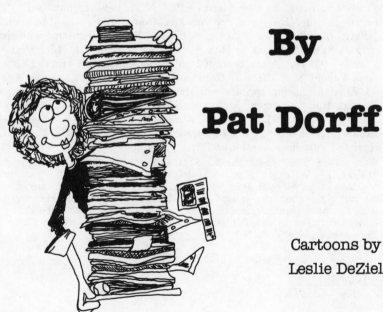

Cartoons by
Leslie DeZiel

St. Martin's Press/New York

Permission to reprint excerpts is gratefully acknowledged:
Mike McGrady, from *The Kitchen Sink Papers — My Life as a Househusband* ©1975 Mike McGrady, reprinted with the permission of Doubleday; Erma Bombeck, from her column in the *Minneapolis Tribune,* ©1982 Erma Bombeck, reprinted with the permission of Aaron M. Priest Literary Agency, Inc.; Richard L. Evans, for his quotation © by Richard L. Evans, reprinted with permission of Richard Evans; Erma Bombeck, from *Aunt Erma's Cope Book* ©1979 Erma Bombeck, reprinted with the permission of Aaron M. Priest Literary Agency, Inc.; Lee Grossman, from *Fat Paper* ©1976 Lee Grossman, reprinted with the permission of McGraw-Hill Book Company; Beryl Pfizer, from "Poor Woman's Almanac," Dec., 1971, *Ladies' Home Journal,* ©1971 Family Media, Inc., reprinted with the permission of *Ladies' Home Journal;* text from Ziggy by Tom Wilson ©1978 Universal Press Syndicate. Reprinted with permission. All rights reserved. Marion Woodman, from *The Owl Was a Baker's Daughter,* ©1980 Marion Woodman, reprinted with the permission of Inner City Books; Dr. Gordon Lawrence, from *People Types and Tiger Stripes,* ©1982 Gordon Lawrence, reprinted with the permission of Dr. Gordon Lawrence; Edwin C. Bliss, from *Getting Things Done: The ABCs of Time Management,* ©1976 Edwin C. Bliss, reprinted with the permission of Charles Scribner's Sons; text from Frank and Ernest by Bob Thaves ©1977 NEA, Inc., reprinted with the permission of NEA, Inc.; Peg Bracken, from "Of Found Money and Related Matters," *Family Circle,* ©1969 Peg Bracken, reprinted with the permission of Peg Bracken; Don Aslett, from *Is There Life After Housework?,* ©1981 Don Aslett, reprinted with the permission of Writer's Digest; Alan Lakein, from *How to Get Control of Your Time and Your Life,* ©1973 Alan Lakein, reprinted with the permission of Reston Pub. Co., a Prentice-Hall Co.; Bonnie McCullough, from *Bonnie's Household Organizer,* ©1980 Bonnie Runyan McCullough, reprinted with permission of Bonnie McCullough; *Dartnell Professional Secretary's Handbook,* ©1971, reprinted with the permission of Dartnell Corp.

Library of Congress Cataloging in Publication Data

    Dorff, Pat.
    File — don't pile!

    Bibliography: p.
    1. Filing systems. I. Title.
HF5736.D67   1986   640'.43   86-6509
ISBN 0-312-28931-6 (pbk.)

Published in the United States of America

Dedicated to
Molly and Amy
the little filers
in
my
family

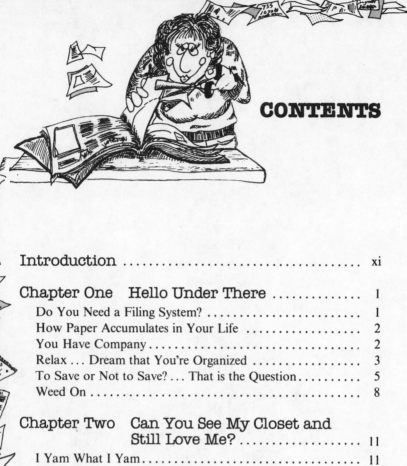

CONTENTS

Acknowledgments

I am grateful to my disorganized friends who attended my filing workshops and encouraged me to get the ideas into written form. I am looking forward to a reunion when I can thank them personally.

I feel the deepest appreciation to Nan and Dick Prince, J. Brent Adair, Paul Wilson, Jr., Jean Heroux, LaNay Davis, and Karen and George Larsgard who believed in me and motivated me. All had the uncanny sense of timing to know when to ask and when not to ask, "How's the book coming?" and never once guffawed at my lofty dream to publish a book.

Many thanks also to Gail Berkey, Diana Hanson, Cathryn Kirkham, Gwynne Smith, Pat Wright, and many others who tended my children. Without their support, I would not have been able to conduct the workshops or to write *File ... Don't Pile!*™ My appreciation to Dr. Carroll Vomhof of the Robbinsdale, Minnesota, School District and to Edith Mucke, Director of the University of Minnesota Continuing Education for Women Program, whose key roles made many File ... Don't Pile workshops available.

I am grateful to Lonnie Bradley, Marcia Handsaker, Merry Franklin, Anna Langford, Jennie Lin Strong, and Louise Plummer for offering their suggestions on the first drafts of the manuscript. I am very grateful to Cindy Piper for editing the final draft and appreciate her willingness to share her time and invaluable advice with me.

For the most delightful cartoons which gave this book life, I owe much to my illustrator and friend, Leslie DeZiel. Special thanks to Maxine George who spent many days on the technical drawings and book design.

Warm thanks to Shirley Dahlen for word processing the manuscript and for enlightening my understanding of the Myers-Briggs Type Indicator.

I especially recognize and express my love and gratitude to my parents, Victor and Florence Morack; and to my sister and brother, Sallie Heise and Donald Morack, and their families. They helped me over so many hurdles it would take another book to record them.

Tremendous credit is due my own little filers, Molly and Amy, who have been with me through thick and thin. They helped tote workshop gear to the car and slept many nights with the vaporizer running (whether they needed it or not) so they wouldn't hear the din of the typewriter. They sat patiently on my lap and by my side as we cut and pasted and read the manuscript over and over. I love them and appreciate them. This book is theirs.

But most of all, I am eternally grateful to the Lord, who gave me the idea in the first place. The idea doesn't belong to me. It's a gift with which I was entrusted. Like a child, it was nurtured and developed. Now, having grown, it is set free to have an influence in others' lives, as it had in mine.

> . . . and so there ain't nothing more to write about, and I am rotten glad of it, because if I'd a knowed what a trouble it was to make a book I wouldn't a tackled it and ain't agoing to no more.

> —Mark Twain, in the conclusion to
> *The Adventures of Huckleberry Finn*

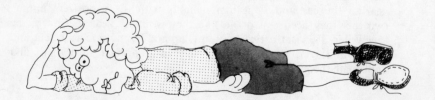

Introduction

The last thing one knows when
writing a book is what to put first.
—Blaise Pascal

I'm a real saver, a bona-fide squirrel. I'm an inveterate clipper of editorials, articles, creative ideas, cartoons, and recipes. You name it, I keep it. In my house, it's a rare magazine or newspaper that is read without scissors in hand.

Friends exchange patterns and quotations with me. I support the photocopy department at Nelson's Office Supply. For years, I've tucked aside brochures and bulletins because I knew somehow somewhere I would be able to use them.

Frankly, I have *always* loved paper. I thrive on it. This began at an early age. As a preschooler, several times a week I corralled every kid on the block into my chicken coop schoolhouse. The most important necessity, of course (next to the blackboard my dad made me), was paper. Plenty of it. From that point on, paper became a genuine weakness. By the time I was in high school, I was clearly an addicted clipaholic. My eyes were like laser beams. They riveted on something in a magazine and out it came.

As a college freshman, I had the best cache of cartoons and ideas in the whole dorm. I also had a roomie who finally drew a line down the middle of the room and refused to talk to me. She was right. My half *was* a pigsty. (I haven't seen her in twenty years. But I'd like to tell her, "Guess what, Jan Rolfs! I no longer have to pole vault into bed!")

Being organized has not always been my forte. I was obviously not born in that condition or I wouldn't have to keep hammering away at it. But I love the idea of being organized. The desire is there. I recognize the pay-offs. I keep trying.

Over the years, I've lived in a variety of apartments, houses, a mobile home, even a cockroach-infested motel room for a time. Wherever I've hung my hat, no matter how much or how little space there was, one common denominator gave it that "homey" appearance. Paper.

I went to great lengths to organize my piles of paper. It always ended in a shifting game. "A" stack would get moved to "B" stack, and "B" to "C." The following Saturday it would all shift back, with very little eliminated in the process. The only time the entire mess was out of sight was before company arrived, when I'd chuck it in grocery bags and shove it in the closet.

The Last Straw

The turning point in my pack-rat life came one day when I opened my closet and a thirty-five foot wave of magazines poured out. I felt frustrated by the mess, not to mention angry at all the time I wasted plowing through boxes crammed with years' worth of treasures. The stuff was stacked up behind the sofa, stashed under the bed and lined the walls of our apartment. (Two weeks after I needed something, I would stumble across it.) Piles and piles of paper controlled me.

I was desperate. I needed *some* kind of filing system. The Big Wave, however, was not the proverbial last straw. It was the sudden decision to move cross country that triggered real action.

I had a substantial investment in magazines and knew my chances of stowing 2,000 pounds of back issues were slim. I had visions of precious information being lost forever if I didn't cull out at least the best articles before the U-Haul arrived. I ripped and stapled like crazy. After I pitched the remnants of the last *Reader's Digest* and *Family Circle*, I looked at the new sea of paper I had created. A hollow feeling crept over me, the kind of feeling that strikes you when you know you've done something irretrievable — like jumping off the high dive for the first time. It dawns on you mid-air you've done a rather gutsy thing, but it's too late to change your mind. I realized then why I hadn't done this before. The articles had been safer in the magazines. The magazine covers were fixed in my brain, and eventually I could find what I wanted. With the covers gone, how could I possibly find a thing?

I needed a filing system fast. (I didn't have any choice — the U-Haul had just backed up to the door.) I wanted something simple, one step beyond the Stash Approach. I picked up a pencil and my first file folder. *Voila!* "Inspiration often follows despair," it's said.

An Idea Is Born

Some years and two moves later, I was visiting with friends who were eager to get themselves organized. They were suffering from my old dilemma. We had an informal lesson on my kitchen table. The word spread, and since that fateful day I've conducted many File ... Don't Pile workshops. It's a practical, flexible, and unbelievably easy system that brings joy and order to people's lives. Almost anyone who can read will be able to use it with little instruction. Children should be able to find information with no difficulty (not to mention knowing where to put it back). This is so important. Files can and should be theirs, too.

My paper predicament has been solved. But I don't want anyone to get the false notion I have now arrived. Be assured, all paper clips do not face east in my house. I have two preschoolers who were born with little scissors in their hands. They smiled up at the doctor and gleefully cut their own umbilical cords. Their scissors have been hot ever since. You can picture the trails that are made each day in our house. It reminds me of Mike McGrady's description in *The Kitchen Sink Papers — My Life as a Househusband:* "Any job that requires six hours to do ... can be undone in six minutes by one small child carrying a plate of crackers and a Monopoly set."

There's Hope, Susie-Save-It-All!

I knew I couldn't possibly be the only clipaholic in the world, but there were two things I didn't realize. Number one, how many serious clippers exist out there, and, number two, how many use the Stash Approach and wish they knew an easy way to file. I surveyed the field. What I found was a ton of stuff on records management for the corporate filer and government documenter. Occasionally, there would be a system geared toward a special audience such as home economics teachers or ministers. But for the general, all-around Susie-Save-It-All and her pack-rat clan, there was zilch. For the small business person who is chief-cook-and-bottle-washer and office clerk, too — yes, you guessed it, zippo. For the volunteer, up to his or her charitable chin in directives and newsletters, there was absolutely nothing. Even the sources specializing in "getting organized" didn't offer a system *per se*.

Some people enjoy chaos. A cluttered desk is comfortable to them. Erma Bombeck claims a clean desk is overrated. She says, "My desk may be 'unstructured,' but I know where everything is. Trust me." Sydney Harris put it this way, "Those proud of keeping an orderly desk never know the thrill of finding something they thought they had irretrievably lost." It *is* a thrill. I know, I've been there!

This book is not for those who have no problems with being messy. It is intended to be a self-teaching guide for those who want a systematic approach on how to organize their papers. What this book has to offer disorganized souls is an easy way to file. It is not a Leaf-Through-It book. It's a Dig-In/Don't-Dabble manual. The book follows the same step by step approach used in the File ... Don't Pile workshop. Once you start organizing your papers, it will be a handy reference source. To derive the most benefit, I suggest you read and use the book in sequence. If you skip around, it will be like darting in and out of class every fifteen minutes or having a disjointed phone conversation with a friend.

I Don't Do Windows ... Yet

What this book does *not* delve into is how to organize anything that isn't paper. Forget the toys, last year's laundry, holiday decorations, sports equipment, photographs, dishes, and so forth. If you need help in solving organizational problems other than paper, I recommend you buy, beg, borrow or bribe any of the titles listed in the bibliography at the end of this book.

Whether the clutter is paper or junk, be assured it's a universal problem. A friend and I traveled to Norway a few years ago. We were very impressed. Our host's home was immaculate, super clean. Everything was neatly in place. It was strange, though. During the entire visit the door next to our room *never* opened. (Since I was on a genealogy trek, I was beginning to wonder if our host had some "family skeletons" in the closet.) It was mysterious. Finally, on the last day of our visit, our hostess, Anna Marie, needed something from The Vault. She apologized over and over as she led us into her *ruske rom* — which in everyone's language is the junk room. Moral: Everyone the world around stashes.

Let's Get Together

Nothing replaces rubbing shoulders with others in the same boat. There's something about seeing people with the same ailment that renews hope. You realize there are others who also feel that simply keeping up with the daily mail would be Utopia.

Such euphoric desires were not far from the mind of one of my students. The first time I taught my workshop at the House of Hope Church in St. Paul, Minnesota, the class was inadvertently scheduled in an upper level room. "The Room at the Top" sounded like a nice place to meet, but it wasn't my idea of a convenient location. Nonetheless, the caravan of women and I packed our gear and trudged upward.

When we got to the third flight of stairs, a sweet elderly woman behind me gasped, "I didn't know we were meeting in heaven for this class." She paused, then said, "But I sure expect to be there when I'm done!"

You may not end up in heaven (or Utopia) after File ... Don't Pile, but you'll be closer. Your group may meet in "The Room at the Top" or "The Room around the Back." It doesn't matter. What counts is the people.

This is your invitation to enroll in a self-help course that will give you a new lease on life. I have hundreds of students who could attest to it. After a week, one woman said, "You changed my life. The television crews for 'That's Incredible' should come to our house!"

None of the ideas in this book will do any good, however, unless *you* apply them. "Itching for what you want doesn't do much good; you've got to scratch for it." Author unknown. (*Apples of Gold* compiled by Jo Petty.) A lot of people wish they were organized. Many people intend to do something about it. They may have *File ... Don't Pile!* on the shelf along with other how-to-books, but until effort is exerted, it is only a vague wish, not a commitment. Hang this quote on the wall in every room. It will inspire you to action:

> *Sooner or later in life comes a time when it is performance that counts — not promises, not possibilities, not potentialities — but performance.... the law of improvement is the law ... of participation, of performance.*
>
> —Richard L. Evans

Do you really want to put your life in order? Paper is only one tiny aspect of it. Don't let it control you. Don't let it gobble up your environment, your time, your money, or your relationship with others. Get control of the paper in your life! DO IT!

Pat Dorff
Minneapolis, Minnesota

File... Don't Pile!™

Chapter One
Hello Under There

Do You Need a Filing System?

Hello under there in Wisconsin, Minnesota, and Iowa! You, too, in California, Utah, and Idaho, Virginia, New York, and Maine! No matter *where* you live — New London, Wisconsin, to Mesa, Arizona, people are plagued by the same dilemma: Paper. Not just paper. PAPER!

It stacks up at work on the desk and the window sills. The file cabinets are crammed, the credenza is full, and the in-basket is overflowing. The nicest part about going home at the end of the day is you don't have to face piles of paper any more. Right? (Except maybe the small load rotting in your briefcase.)

"Home, sweet home,"where the stuff is piled high on the refrigerator, the cupboards, and the hutch. The last time the dresser top showed was five years ago, when it arrived from the store. What isn't on the dining room table is stashed out of sight under the bed and in the closets. Erma Bombeck wasn't kidding when she asked, "Can you open your closet door without hurting yourself?" (She should have been around the day a ton of magazines nearly put me in traction.)

Some poor souls wallow in paper day *and* night because their offices are *in* their homes. It's impossible to escape the stacks of brochures, financial records, client data, and mail generated daily from owning a small business or cottage industry. In addition, these people cope with accumulations of how-to booklets, pamphlets, and magazine articles concerning the operation of a small business. They deal with the paper in one way or another: 1) Ignoring it. (It doesn't go away.) 2) Ranting around the house until they find what they need. (The missing papers don't always surface, but sometimes the neighbors do!) or 3) Getting rid of it. (They hide it, chuck it, or, in rare cases, somehow file it.)

While most of the examples cited in this book are focused on personal papers, the filing system can be adapted to organize business-related papers as well. Other kinds of papers — for instance, those papers concerning political or community involvement, administration of an organization, and committee work — can also be organized according to the methods taught in this book.

How Paper Accumulates in Your Life

Let's face it, this is a paper-oriented society. It was twenty-five years ago. Despite technology, it still is. Lee Grossman agrees. In his book, *Fat Paper*, he says,

> If modern technology were the answer to the paperwork explosion we would have solved it by now. On the contrary, the reverse has been true. Modern technology has merely given us the ability to turn out paper faster and faster; how we've used this ability has been another matter. Unfortunately, all too often the results have been fat paper. Everyone suffers from fat paper.

Some paper enters your life quite innocently. It isn't solicited. Your children, your spouse, and you bring home pounds of pulp because it's necessary for school, work, or organizations. The mailman delivers a wad daily. In 1984 alone, U.S. postal carriers delivered more than forty-eight billion pieces of circulars or third-class mail. That figure is staggering, and it's on the increase each year.

However, most paper doesn't come through the door so innocently. It is deliberately invited. Your children, your spouse, and you pick it up, clip it out, copy it over, and mail for reams of stuff in all shapes and sizes. Notes and reminders, lists, and even lists of lists are created. Beryl Pfizer once admitted in the *Ladies' Home Journal,* "I write down everything I want to remember. That way, instead of spending a lot of time trying to remember what it is I wrote down, I spend the time looking for the paper I wrote it down on."

You Have Company

Why people glom onto paper and clutter their lives with it is a separate issue. That is discussed in the next chapter. *Who* are these people who are inundated with paper? Don't delude yourself into thinking your problem with paper is unique. You have company from all walks of life, all ages, in every money bracket and marital status, male or female, with or without children. The Ph.D. (Piled-high-and-Deep) desk can belong to *anybody.*

Let's imagine you are in an actual File ... Don't Pile workshop. Look around you. Who else is in class? (You know your sister should be here — but she signed up for Speed Reading, Time Management, and Quicky Cuisine and couldn't squeeze it in.)

There is a new bride with a shoebox full of recipes all neatly copied and clipped. (She wants to get her marriage off to a good start.) The lady next to her is unpacking twenty years of spelling papers and artwork from her eight children (along with a smudged recipe for "Chocolate Elephant Tracks" which has been missing since her Harold was in third grade).

At the next table, an older man is sifting through a big stack of yellowed clippings on architecture and historical sites. Sitting next to him is his wife who has a mound of sewing patterns and articles. A woman arrives carrying an armload of bulging envelopes — her method, until now, of filing her gardening tips.

On the other side of the room, a woman has just removed her furs and is fingering an array of beautifully photographed brochures about the Far East. Another is adjusting her maternity top and is about to tackle a make-do file box jammed with craft ideas from recycled macaroni.

One person is complaining that her family thought moving into their larger home last year would help them get organized. Instead they have just accumulated more! Someone coming in the door remarks, "You think you have problems! We're moving next week from a six-bedroom home into a condo." She's consoled (slightly) by a lady struggling with the thought of dealing with her deceased mother's estate. No will. Nothing marked. Nothing pitched in fifty years.

It's a composite picture. They're all there. Do any of them seem like someone you know?

I've worked with people at varying levels of disorder. Some border on lost cause; with others, it's a survival of the fittest. Still others, fanatically organized, cannot find a thing. Like the people in this composite, only you, dear Reader, know what degree of chaos your papers are in and how you would like them to be. If you find yourself saying, "This isn't the end of the earth, but I can see it from here," take heart. Even if you are among those who spy registration material in the garbage three days after you miss the first day of class, there's hope.

Relax ... Dream that You're Organized

First, let's dream for a little while. Dream that all your papers, wherever they are piled, are already neatly filed. They aren't just stashed. They are *organized*. If you're sitting in the middle of a big mess while you're reading this, it may be hard to imagine. Remove yourself to a favorite local deli for hot apple pie and cinnamon ice cream, or grab a lemonade and sunbathe for a while. Pretend you are organized. Imagine being able to walk into any room in the middle of the night, lights out, without tripping over a box. There isn't a shred of clutter to be seen.

What about tomorrow? Won't there be more paper? You bet your sweet scissors there will be. As sure as the sun rises, paper is going to keep pouring into your life. It isn't going to quit coming just because you are all caught up on your filing today.

What criteria do you use to determine whether or not you should acquire a piece of paper? An all-time high excuse sounds like this: "Oh, is that FREE? Great, I'll take ten — one is for my neighbor, one for my sister-in-law — and I better have two (in case I lose one)...." Another biggie is the It-looks-good, it-must-be-good line of thinking. Many magazine articles, brochures, and pamphlets have great eye appeal. They are bright and splashy, colorful and glossy-slick. They are a temptation for even the most self-disciplined saver. If something is free *and* attractive, who can resist? Why do you suppose plastic-handled bags are distributed at conventions and exhibits? You are *expected* to take home an armload.

The Crowning Glory of reasons people hang onto stuff is the belief in five little words: "I might need that someday." Those famous last words were probably the rule, rather than the exception, for many pioneers loading their wagons. I wouldn't be surprised if they were echoed many times on the Ark before Noah closed the door, too.

If these are the only reasons you keep a piece of paper, it isn't any wonder piles accumulate. Concentrate for a few minutes on the paper

that will come into your life today and tomorrow, henceforth and forever. Think only about the new paper. Remember, since you're still dreaming, your papers from the past twenty years are already filed. The answer to what to save in the future should be based on several criteria.

To Save or Not to Save? ... That Is the Question

When I attended library school, I received a handout listing ten questions for evaluating books. Over the years I've forgotten from whom I received the questions (a painful reminder of my disorganized past), but I have not forgotten how invaluable the questions were in my professional work.

The ten basic criteria for selecting and saving books also apply to paperwork. Obviously, not every piece of paper will meet all ten criteria. But get into the habit of asking yourself these questions whenever any paper comes through your hands.

1. Do I really WANT it?

Although this question appears to be simplistic, papers often pile up because the issue isn't considered important. When it is faced honestly, a lot of paper can be eliminated from our lives. Ask yourself, "Do I really *want* this pattern?", "Do I really *want* this article on fighting inflation?", "Do I really *want* this pamphlet on potty training a child?" If you don't want it, then don't cut it out, don't send for it just because it's a freebie or don't take it home from the doctor's office. Get rid of it, if you don't want it. Throw it away. Give it to someone else and let it be his problem.

2. Do I NEED it?

You may not especially want to keep a certain piece of paper, but sometimes it's a necessity. You *need* to hang onto it. It may be a document of some nature or an application form or an unpaid bill or a coupon worth a 30% discount. There are many papers you may only need to keep for a short duration and others you *need* to retain for the rest of your life. If you can state, "Yes, I *need* this piece of paper," in questioning its value, then it warrants keeping it.

3. Will it ADD SOMETHING NEW to the material already on hand?

Perhaps the easiest way to illustrate the importance of this question is to ask another question. If you have a cooking file, do you *really* need ten carrot cake recipes? Files can become cluttered too. Unless information provides a new viewpoint or a different creative slant to that which is already on hand, file drawers will overflow with redundancy. A spinoff of this problem is the person who saves multiple copies of papers for future use or to share with others. This can be legitimate, depending on your answers to questions four and five.

4. Is it SIGNIFICANT FOR MY PURPOSES?

One of my clients had a wealth of information on any subject you could imagine. Nan was literally the resource person for the neighborhood. Everyone knew she would have a poem, pattern, quote, recipe, whatever, for any occasion. She often saved certain papers with specific people in mind.

If the purpose of your file is to provide a resource tool for a specific group, this is fine. You may be a leader in the Girl Scouts and as such need a file of ideas. It is significant for that purpose. If you are a Red Cross swim instructor or operate a nursery school or are a free lance decorator, you need to maintain a file of ideas with many people in mind. That is your purpose. If your file, however, is to serve only those within the family circle, don't save material unless it's significant for the needs of your family.

5. Do I FORESEE A USE for it?

The I-might-need-that-someday crutch many people lean on was worded this way in a Ziggy cartoon: "I figure it's better to have it, and not need it . . . than to need it, and not have it!" If you can *foresee a use* for a piece of paper, however — not just have a vague notion that you might use it — it warrants keeping it.

Several years ago I saw a darling dollhouse pattern in *Family Circle* magazine. It nearly jumped off the page, it was so cute. In a flash, I had the pattern ripped out, stapled and the dollhouse half-built in my mind. Never mind the fact I didn't have any children. My thinking was: If I ever have a baby, and if that baby is a girl, and if Grandpa is willing to make it, I'd love to have this little dollhouse for her. I did, and she was, and he did, and we have it. The dollhouse is delightful. I'm so glad I saved the pattern because I knew that was what I wanted. At some point, however, if I didn't have any girls, I would have had to admit no to questions 1 through 5 and give the pattern to someone with daughters. (It was much too nice to simply throw away.)

6. Is it TIMELY?

Anyone who has been out of the professional work force for ten years quickly realizes how much new data is produced in a short span of time. Information in your files should be kept current, unless you're writing an historical account. (Or you're nostalgia-minded.)

Some papers don't seem to date as fast as others. However, with new products always coming on the market, needlework, home repair, and recipe files are not exempt from becoming outdated either.

You'll find it much easier to keep materials up-to-date, if you —
ALWAYS DATE AND SOURCE EACH ITEM.

Whether it's an article from *Psychology Today* or a folk art pattern, always indicate the date and source on the item. Most magazines cite this information on the bottom of each page. If it is material you have acquired from a friend, write, for example: "From Jane Jellings, Mpls., MN, Nov., 1980."

7. Is it QUALITY?

Quality is a very personal matter. I respect and appreciate the individual differences that result in answering this question. What is quality to you may not be to Bev Murphy who lives down the street. What appears to be a worthless yellowed newspaper clipping to one person, may be a priceless gem to another. The old adage, "One person's trash is another person's treasure," couldn't be more applicable.

Answering yes to the quality question doesn't necessarily mean comparing another person's opinion with yours. It involves deciding for yourself whether or not an item is valuable. I've learned over many years of clipping and saving that I've become more selective, more discriminating. Like Anne Morrow Lindbergh, in *Gift from the Sea,* whose pockets bulged with wet shells she greedily collected, my files exploded in growth. When I developed more quality control, I no longer saved everything that wasn't nailed down. A paper should have something more than merely being on the subject of your interest. It must be quality.

8. Is it ACCURATE and RELIABLE?

A few years ago a man of a different faith asked me why my church engaged in a particular activity. I was stunned by his question. I knew his assumption was incorrect. When I clarified the information, he was appalled by how the writer of the article he had read had misconstrued the facts.

Certainly you cannot take the time to investigate every author's research. You rely on the reputation of the publication to report facts which are accurate. You do not want to clutter your files with information that is in doubt.

The next question is closely related and is a helpful determiner.

9. Is the AUTHOR AN AUTHORITY on the subject?

It may not matter to some whether Billy Casper authors an article on French cooking or Julia Child writes about golf. Presumably, however, most golfers and most cooks would prefer reading information written by an authority in the field. When learning about an unfamiliar religion, it's preferable to have an authority of that faith relate the beliefs, rather than to have an authority of another faith speculate on it.

Popular subjects of the day (bandwagon topics) are breeding ground for pseudoauthoritative documentaries. Does the author sound like he knows what he is writing about? People can become expert in more than one subject area, but credibility should be established in each area.

10. Is it EASY TO UNDERSTAND?

When saving papers, it is as relevant to consider who uses the file as it is to consider their level of understanding. Is the material meant to benefit a younger member of the family writing a school report about the Viking raiders? A brochure about the archeological finds of Norwegian Vikings may be free and look good and may pass the test on all of the above nine questions. But, if the information is too technical to be understood, it isn't a valuable addition to your file.

Although I am interested in photography, saving an article on "Lens Attachments for Color Telephoto Picture Taking" would be extraneous. On the other hand, "The Anatomy of Migration: from Europe to the U.S. in the Nineteenth Century" is a viable resource for a genealogy bug like me.

You can place an immediate value judgment on a piece of paper by recognizing the degree of interest and understanding of those who will use the information.

BONUS: 11. Can I OBTAIN IT ELSEWHERE?

Ask yourself if keeping *National Geographic* back to 1955 is really worth the cost of storage. Consider how frequently you refer to them. Then ask yourself whether you can obtain the information elsewhere when it's needed. Public, private, university, church and company libraries are great resources accessible by telephone.

Weed On ...

Okay, pop that dream! It was nice while it lasted. The truth is, the paper is still there, piled high and waiting to be organized.

The ten questions are great. They will help you eliminate a lot of paper accumulating in the future. But perhaps you are thinking, "It's the twenty years worth of stuff parked all over this joint I'm concerned about." Of course! You wouldn't have purchased this book if you (or your mother or uncle or sister if it's for them) didn't have stacks of papers and magazines to organize.

The same ten questions apply to the *past* twenty years' accumulation, as well as what comes through the door tomorrow. You can weed out a lot of paper before you actually use my method of filing. It will save you time, money and space in the end. Later in the book, I'll show you ways to determine how long to retain papers and how you can periodically weed papers you have filed.

The ten questions are a guideline that will help you in two ways: 1) to control your intake of new paper, and 2) to seize control over the paper you already have. Whenever you have a piece of paper in your hand, ask yourself these questions over and over. Make it an unconscious habit to ask, "Do I want this?" "Do I need this?" "Is this significant for my purposes?" One person denied the value of these questions. Yet, as we were going through a box of her materials I overheard her mumbling, "Oh, here's that cartoon I've been looking for. Gee, I wonder, do I really *want* this any more? I guess I don't *need* it."

Some people find the first question, "Do I really WANT it?" a little absurd. Their response is typically, "Of course, I *want* this recipe. I *want* every recipe in print. That's why I've got such a mess!" It is often very difficult for them to admit, "I don't *need* another carrot cake recipe." There are probably many explanations *why* people accumulate and clutter their lives with paper. One possibility is to explore the field of human personality. Are certain personality types more prone to save paper and others, to pitch it? Chapter Two presents the perspective that psychology provides in understanding *why* people act the way they do concerning paperwork and filing.

Summary

Ten Questions to Determine Whether or Not to Save a Piece of Paper

1. Do I *want* it?
2. Do I *need* it?
3. Will it *add something new?*
4. Is it *significant for my purposes?*
5. Do I *foresee a use* for it?
6. Is it *timely?*
7. Is it *quality?*
8. Is it *accurate and reliable?*
9. Is the *author an authority* on the subject?
10. Is it *easy to understand?*

Bonus: 11. Can I *obtain it elsewhere?*

Chapter Two
Can You See My Closet and Still Love Me?

I Yam What I Yam

Have you ever wondered why your sister is never late to a meeting —while you do well to remember the *day* of the meeting?

Do you sometimes wonder why your best friend can have every recipe at her fingertips — while you rearrange yours monthly and still can't find the one for your favorite cream puff?

Do you occasionally wonder why your spouse or roommate doesn't appreciate the importance of your boxes of papers stashed in the closet — when their value is so obvious to you?

There are more questions than answers to why people accumulate paper and find it difficult to manage. Of all the questions, the following eight are the most often repeated in File ... Don't Pile workshops.

1. Why do some people have a need to collect and save everything while others can easily throw papers away?
2. Why do some people find more difficulty than others in knowing where to file papers?
3. Why are some people gung ho when starting to file, and fizzle in midstream, but others follow through to the end?
4. Why do some people get sidetracked and distracted when filing, while others stay on course?
5. Why do some people need an uninterrupted block of time before they can start filing, and others can file when they have bits and pieces of time?
6. Why do some people seldom return items to file drawers after they're used, and others always put papers back?
7. Why do some people always seek more ideas on how to get

organized, but seldom use any of them, while others implement new ideas and move forward?

8. Why do some people have a need to change others to their way of organizing, while other people can appreciate their opposites?

I cannot offer conclusive answers to these questions. The purpose of this chapter is to create an awareness of some reasons *why* people act the way they do concerning paperwork and filing. As Marion Woodman writes in her book, *The Owl Was a Baker's Daughter,* "Consciousness will not always solve the problem, but it may make the suffering meaningful."

Sixteen Ways to View the World

I am not a psychologist. I am an observer. It seemed to me from my observations of hundreds of File ... Don't Pile workshop participants that psychology might provide a perspective on the eight common questions about paper control. One day a student in a workshop acquainted me with the fascinating field of Jungian typology, a way of understanding human personality. My introduction came via a highly successful and reliable psychometric inventory, the Myers-Briggs Type Indicator (MBTI). My understanding of the MBTI was greatly increased in my reading of *Gifts Differing,* by Isabel Briggs Myers and *People Types and Tiger Stripes,* by Dr. Gordon Lawrence and in conversations with Dr. Lawrence and Shirley Dahlen, an MBTI consultant.

The MBTI was created by Ms. Myers and her mother, Katharine C. Briggs, after twenty years of exhaustive research and development. Their intention in developing their instrument was to measure the attitudes and functions of people's personalities as defined by Swiss psychiatrist C. G. Jung.

According to the theory of Jungian typology, people experience the world in one of two basic attitudes: 1) as *Extraverts,* with the energy of their lives flowing primarily outward, or 2) as *Introverts,* with the energy of their lives flowing primarily inward. People also have preferences among the basic functions: the Perceptive function includes the *Sensation* process, which tells that something exists and the *Intuitive* process, which tells where something is going; the Judgment functions include the *Thinking* process, which tells what something is and the *Feeling* process, which tells what something is worth.

The following chart indicates the implications of preferences for each of the attitudes and functions as well as the choice of using either the perceptive function or the judgment function in the outer lives.

1. E EXTRAVERSION
   Relates more easily to the outer world of actions, objects, and persons than to the inner world of ideas.

   or I INTROVERSION
   Relates more easily to the inner world of ideas than to the outer world of actions, objects, and persons.

2. S SENSING
   Prefers working with known facts more than possibilities and relationships.

   or N*INTUITION
   Prefers looking for possibilities and relationships than working with known facts.

3. T THINKING
   Bases judgments more on impersonal analysis and logic than on values.

   or F FEELING
   Bases judgments more on personal values than on impersonal analysis and logic.

4. J JUDGMENT
   Likes a planned, decided, orderly way of life better than a flexible, spontaneous way.

   or P PERCEPTION
   Likes a flexible, spontaneous way of life better than a planned, decided, orderly way.

* The letter, "N," represents Intuition since the letter, "I," is used for Introversion.

The concept of psychological types can be approached on many different levels. The Myers-Briggs Type Indicator presents sixteen possible ways of seeing the world — with many variables even within each type. Jungian analysts and therapists, as well as others trained in the professional use of the MBTI, see typology as one of many factors which account for behavior. They do not use type to "label" persons or "to put them in boxes," but to help them understand each individual as a complex person with unique characteristics.

This chapter is an application of typology as it relates to the ways people get organized and their patterns of motivation. Although this application is intentionally simplified, it provides a framework for exploring new possibilities.

What are Your Preferences?

The beginning of understanding why others act the way they do is first to understand who *you* are. In a limited way, the following exercise will help you to identify your personality type. On the next eight pages are brief checklists adapted from *People Types and Tiger Stripes,* by Dr. Gordon Lawrence. Put a check mark opposite each phrase that comfortably describes you. As you do this exercise, keep this statement from the MBTI in mind:

"Whatever your preferences ... you may still use some behaviors characteristic of contrasting preferences, *but not with equal liking or skill."* (emphasis added)

If you are an EXTRAVERT, it is likely you would:

_____ choose to work with others, with large groups.

_____ plunge into new experiences, working by trial and error.

_____ be relaxed and confident.

_____ readily talk over events and ideas with others.

_____ be interested in other people and their doings.

_____ readily offer opinions.

_____ share personal experiences.

_____ want to experience things so as to understand them.

_____ be enthusiastic about activities involving action.

_____ ask questions to check on the expectations of the group or teacher.

_____ have a relatively short attention span.

_____ dislike complicated procedures and get impatient with slow jobs.

_____ be interested in the results of the job, in getting it done, and in how other people do it.

_____ eagerly attend to interruptions.

_____ act quickly, sometimes without thinking.

_____ like to have people around.

_____ communicate well and greet people easily.

If you are an INTROVERT, it is likely you would:

_____ choose to work alone or with one person.

_____ hold back from new experiences.

_____ choose written assignments over oral presentations.

_____ perform better in written work than in oral presentations.

_____ pause before answering, and show discomfort with spontaneous questioning.

_____ ask questions to allow understanding something before attempting to do it.

_____ be hard to understand, quiet and shy; seem "deep."

_____ be intense, bottling up emotions.

_____ prefer setting your own standards when possible.

_____ go from considering to doing and back to considering.

_____ have a small number of carefully selected friends.

_____ like quiet space to work.

_____ work intently on the task at hand.

_____ work on one thing for a long time.

_____ prefer jobs that can be done "inside the head."

_____ dislike interruptions.

_____ like to think a lot before action, sometimes not acting at all.

If you prefer SENSING, it is likely you would:

_____ be realistic and practical.

_____ be intensely aware of the environment.

_____ be more observant than imaginative.

_____ be pleasure loving and contented.

_____ be possessive of things, a consumer.

_____ be imitative; prefer memorizing rather than finding out reasons.

_____ change moods as physical surroundings change.

_____ learn best from an orderly progression of sequential details.

_____ bring up pertinent facts.

_____ keep accurate track of details, make lists.

_____ be patient.

_____ be good at checking, inspecting, "reading the fine print," and precise work.

_____ dislike new problems unless there are standard ways to solve them.

_____ like an established routine.

_____ enjoy using skills already learned more than learning new ones.

_____ work steadily all the way through to a conclusion, not having bursts of energy and slack periods.

_____ be impatient or frustrated with complicated situations.

_____ not usually get inspirations and not trust inspirations.

If you prefer INTUITION, it is likely you would:

_____ crave inspiration.

_____ be more imaginative than observant.

_____ pay more attention to the whole concept than to details.

_____ be aware of only the personally relevant aspects of the external environment.

_____ become restless, impatient with routines.

_____ be an initiator, promoter, inventor of ideas.

_____ see possibilities that others miss.

_____ be quick with finding solutions.

_____ not always "hear others out," tend to interrupt others.

_____ be indifferent to what others own or consume.

_____ look far ahead; furnish new ideas.

_____ like spotting problems and solving them.

_____ dislike doing the same thing over.

_____ enjoy learning a new skill more than using it.

_____ work in bursts of energy and have slack periods in between.

_____ jump to conclusions; make factual errors.

_____ dislike taking time for precision.

_____ follow inspirations good or bad.

If you prefer THINKING, it is likely you would:

_____ be logical and analytical.

_____ be impersonal, impartial.

_____ be more interested in ideas or things than in human relationships.

_____ be more truthful than tactful.

_____ be stronger in executive ability than in the social arts.

_____ be brief and businesslike.

_____ take very seriously facts, theories, and the discovery of truth.

_____ take seriously the solution of practical problems.

_____ treat emotional relationships and ideals quite casually.

_____ contribute intellectual criticism.

_____ expose wrongs in the habits, customs, and beliefs of others.

_____ be offended by illogic in others.

_____ hold firmly to a policy or conviction.

_____ hurt other people's feelings without knowing it.

_____ not need harmony.

_____ decide things impersonally, sometimes ignoring people's wishes.

_____ be upset by injustice.

_____ not seem to know how your own actions affect other people's feelings.

If you prefer FEELING, it is likely you would:

_____ be personal, like personal relationships.

_____ be more interested in people than in things or ideas.

_____ be more tactful than truthful, if forced to choose.

_____ be likely to agree with others in the group.

_____ think as others think, believing them probably right.

_____ find it difficult to be brief and businesslike.

_____ take emotional relationships and ideals very seriously.

_____ be offended by a lack of personal consideration in others.

_____ be motivated by others.

_____ be compliant.

_____ permit feelings to override logic.

_____ forecast how others will feel.

_____ arouse enthusiasm.

_____ be upset by conflicts; value harmony.

_____ dislike telling people unpleasant things.

_____ relate well to most people.

_____ be sympathetic.

If you are JUDGING, it is likely you would:

_____ have your mind made up.

_____ be more decisive than curious.

_____ live according to plans.

_____ live according to standards and customs not easily or lightly set aside.

_____ try to make situations conform to your own standards, "the way they ought to be."

_____ make definite choices from among the possibilities.

_____ be uneasy with unplanned happenings.

_____ base friendship upon beliefs, standards, and tastes which are assumed to be shared.

_____ have enduring friendships.

_____ see more perceptive people as aimless drifters, unmoral if not immoral.

_____ aim to be right.

_____ be self-regulated, purposeful, and exacting.

_____ be orderly, organized, and systematic.

_____ persevere.

_____ have settled opinions.

_____ be tolerant of routine.

If you are PERCEPTIVE, it is likely you would:

_____ be more curious than decisive.

_____ live according to the situation of the moment.

_____ not be likely to plan things but would act spontaneously.

_____ be masterful in handling the unplanned, unexpected, or incidental.

_____ be empirical and dependent on experience.

_____ amass vast quantities of experiences, more than can be digested or used.

_____ be uncritical.

_____ base friendships on accessibility and shared experience.

_____ easily and often drop friendships, forget them, resume them.

_____ aim to miss nothing.

_____ be flexible, adaptable, and tolerant.

_____ be understanding and open-minded.

_____ leave things open.

_____ have trouble making decisions.

_____ start too many projects and have difficulty in finishing them.

_____ postpone unpleasant jobs.

_____ welcome new light on a thing, situation, or person.

When you have completed the checklists, compare the tallies of E and I, S and N, T and F, and J and P. By combining your four preferences (i.e., ESFJ), you have an *estimation* of your personality type.

The concept of psychological type is only *one* of many factors, however, that may account for your attitudes and behaviors about organization. How your childhood home was organized, for instance, has an impact on your adult life. If you grew up with adults who had a system that was neat and orderly, you at least observed one organized system. If no one in your family used an orderly system, you may have no pattern for orderliness. Your childhood environment may have nurtured and encouraged you to use your preferred style, or it may have discouraged you by negating your natural way. Your natural style of organization may or may not be the same as others in the family. Like plants, people thrive in the particular environment that meets their needs.

Personality Type and Paper Control

My awareness of the MBTI and Jungian typology made me curious about the relationship between personality type and paper control. Let's review the eight questions on paper control presented at the beginning of this chapter. This time, however, a notation about type is added to show how it may affect paper control. Characteristics most likely to be true for persons in each category are also given.

1. Who are those people who have a need to collect and "save everything," ...
FEELING/PERCEPTIVE
Characteristics: They have full garages, full attics, and bulging purses. They have every birthday card they have ever received. Their philosophy is "I might need that someday," and they would rather postpone judgment.
... and who are those who can easily throw papers away?
THINKING/JUDGING
Characteristics: Having already decided the worth or utility of a thing, they throw away old magazines, announcements, letters, and other papers that don't fit their present categories. They will probably leave little for others to clean up after they die.

2. Who are those people who find difficulty in knowing where to file papers, ...
✓ PERCEPTIVE
Characteristics: Because they are not ready to decide just how to use the papers, they don't want to permanently fix them in a category and thus limit the potential uses. Without clearly defined categories, they

can't decide in which category it should be filed, and they don't know where the file should be stored.

... and who are those who know just where papers belong?

JUDGING

Characteristics: They have clearly defined categories and know exactly what they want to save, which categories to use, and where they should store the file.

3. Who are those people who are gung ho when starting to file — and then fizzle in midstream, ...

✓ INTUITIVE

Characteristics: They lose momentum after papers are centralized. They have boxes lined up in the basement for six months. They are easily sidetracked by a new idea. Beginnings are much more interesting than maintaining the uninspired routines of what they have already collected.

... and who are those who follow through to the end?

SENSING

Characteristics: They plan time for a filing project and actually do the filing. They make filing a priority until the project is completed. For them, having facts and resources organized and at hand is an important part of knowing who they are and to what they are best suited.

4. Who are those people who get sidetracked and distracted when filing, ...

✓ INTUITIVE

Characteristics: They stop to read a magazine article or a nostalgic letter in the midst of cleaning a closet. They would eagerly interrupt their filing project to fetch a box of magazines their neighbor just threw away. Fascination with immediacy calls them away from mundane things that have lost the sparkle of newness.

... and who are those who stay on course?

SENSING

Characteristics: They would set aside a Wednesday morning to file — and would do it. They have a *task* at hand, specifically, cleaning the closet, and would save a nostalgic letter for reading at a later time.

5. Who are those who feel they need an uninterrupted block of time before they can start filing, ...

✓ INTUITIVE AND/OR FEELING

Characteristics: Believing that they may need to change the filing categories, they fear having another unfinished project, so they don't want to begin. They anticipate the project to be more complicated than it is. When they try filing in bits and pieces of time, they find they can't finish because they have so many interests.

...and who are those who can file when they have bits and pieces of time?
EXTRAVERT/THINKING
Characteristics: They can work on projects in bits and pieces because they can "keep six balls going in the air" simultaneously. They can usually find an uninterrupted block of time to file because they plan ahead for it. They experience time differently — as bits of time strung together.

6. Who are those people who seldom return items to file drawers after they're used, ...
✓ INTUITIVE/PERCEPTIVE
Characteristics: They have many interests and enjoy involvement. They are much less interested in following through with things, such as cleaning up, putting things away, or shutting cupboard doors. They enjoy the variety of interruptions.

...and who are those who always put papers back?
SENSING/JUDGING
Characteristics: They can't stand having a mess. They like neat desks. They want their resources located, organized, and accessible.

7. Who are those people who always seek more ideas on how to get organized, but seldom use any of them, ...
✓ INTUITIVE
Characteristics: They seek a filing system and find *File ... Don't Pile* (and other systems), but seldom get around to using any of them. They often collect and save articles on how to get organized, but are more interested in the ideas than in the chores of putting it into their habit system.

...and who are those who implement new ideas and move forward?
SENSING
Characteristics: They seek a filing system, find it, and use it — and are grateful that somebody worked out the system for them.

8. Who are those who feel they need to change others to their way of organizing, ...
May be ANY of the types
Characteristics: They have difficulty in understanding why others are the way they are. They feel their own ways are correct or feel jealous of their opposites and put others down.

...and who are those who can appreciate their opposites?
May be ANY of the types
Characteristics: They either understand and accept themselves and others or appear accepting when it is really indifference.

From the descriptions just cited, it appears that the only "organized" persons are those whose preferences include the *Sensing* (S) or *Thinking* (T) processes and/or those who prefer to use their *Judgment* (J) function in their outer lives. If this is true, how do the people get organized who prefer the *Intuitive* (N) and *Feeling* (F) processes and/or who prefer to use their *Perceptive* (P) function in their outer lives? I discussed this at length with a friend whose type is Introverted Feeling with Intuition (INFP). Her response was meaningful and should be helpful to many who prefer the NFP style. She says:

> I've always had trouble getting organized, deciding where things should be placed — and especially returning things after I've used them. Unless I need to get ready for a dinner or a party, I'm usually only dimly aware that my house is a mess. When I have a deadline for a party, however, my attention is focused on my guests. The anticipation motivates me to work quickly and efficiently. *My feeling is involved.* I've been existing this way for years. I just didn't know *why* I functioned this way. The information provided by the MBTI helped me tremendously to understand myself. Unless something is personally relevant, I don't pay much attention to it. True! It isn't until I need the space on the kitchen counter to bake a cake that I clear off the piles of papers. It isn't until I have company coming that I see a need to pick up clutter in the living room. Then I use the Stash Approach.
>
> By studying typology and the MBTI, I have learned that the "ESTJ" side of my personality is my "inferior" side or the "shadow" side. That's the part of me that functions more slowly, is more primitive, and often acts as the "fool." I've learned that I cannot "demand" it, but that I need to treat it with respect. Paradoxically, this is also the place of some of my best "gifts."
>
> It was very helpful to attend a File . . . Don't Pile workshop and discover a system that *works.* Knowing the techniques, however, doesn't automatically motivate me to get the job done! I need the help and encouragement of others, as well as patience with myself.

Type Makes a Difference

The title of this chapter asks, "Can you see my closet and still love me?" Look at the closet illustrated in Chapter Three and rephrase the question: "Can you know what I'm *really* like and still accept me?" Our closets, our files, and our kitchens often become visible symbols of our lives — and, therefore, provide the focal point for conflicts.

The theory of personality type goes beyond clarifying the answers to the eight questions on paper control. *Knowledge of typology* can increase an awareness of oneself as well as an understanding of relationships with others. It provides clues which will suggest the most effective way for each of us to learn the *skills* which we need for everyday living. A by-product, too, is the fresh perspective this knowledge provides in solving problems, choosing a career, managing a business, teaching students — even in relating to one's "weaknesses."

Psychologists and educators have spent many years of research carefully developing the psychological type theory. The interpretation of the MBTI inventory and counseling based on the results should be provided by persons qualified by training and experience. The MBTI is being used increasingly by educators, psychologists, therapists, psychoanalysts, management consultants, and career counselors. If you would like more information concerning psychological type, either contact me (see Step 5 below) or contact the Center for Applications of Psychological Type, 2720 N.W. 6th Street, Gainesville, FL 32601, for a list of printed material about type or for the names and addresses of resource persons in your area.

In this chapter, I have shared one perspective which can be helpful in coping with clutter. I am interested in providing a system for helping people control paper clutter, but I am also interested in having people *use* the system. Like Isabel Briggs Myers, I dream that "long after I'm gone, my work will go on helping others."

Summary
Five Steps to Understanding More About Your Organizational Style

Step 1. Determine your preferences to estimate your personality type.

Step 2. Compare the tallies of E and I, S and N, T and F, and J and P, and combine your preferences (for example, INFJ or ES/NFP).

Step 3. Review the eight questions on paper control, and identify the characteristics most like you.

Step 4. Take your type into account as you deal with yourself and other people, and validate it with your experience.

Step 5. Write to Pat Dorff at Willowtree Press, 8108 33rd Pl. N., Minneapolis, MN 55427, if you would like more information concerning psychological type as it relates to getting organized.

Chapter Three
Okay, Let's Minimize the Mess

More Reasons Why Paperwork Doesn't Get Organized

There are two universal reasons offered by many people who have difficulty getting beyond the "intention" stage of organizing their mess of papers. One reason is that **it's never the right time.** They wait for the vernal equinox to put them in the mood. When spring finally arrives, the very last place they feel like burying their heads is deep in some closet. The garden beckons. The yardwork starts yelling. They break for the door repeating their Summer Motto: "Once the kids are in school, I'll hit the closets. There will be plenty of time before the holidays to get my act together." (The leaves, of course, automatically vacuum themselves up.) I can relate to this. There was a point in my life when I never spring cleaned. I just moved!

It's a vicious circle. I call it THE SEASONAL BY-PASS SYNDROME. It produces only one thing — Gnawing Guilt. Gnawing Guilt is an uncomfortable condition that is generally alleviated by employing hired help. Or by loudly proclaiming, "It's not lack of ambition, it's lack of *time!* No wonder this joint always looks like Hannibal's elephants are camping out in the hall closet!"

The second reason is **lack of know-how.** Most people aren't quite sure *how* to file. They attack their piles of papers like they often do their closets. In one fell swoop on Fed-up-to-Here-Day, it all comes out of the closet and onto the floor. The closet is swabbed out. A few neatly labeled boxes are stacked on the shelf. A feeling of industry and accomplishment prevails. Then the phone rings. After the call, a little more gets pitched or packed away. In midstream, some long forgotten letter or magazine is unearthed, and two hours disappear in nostalgic joy. A horrified glance at the clock sets off a panic. It's time to be here or there or to get dinner ready. Stash, stuff, save! It all goes back in! The closet is worse off than it was before.

Many people have related to this description of closet clutter. One of my students particularly identified with having sacks in the closet. She even had a name for hers. She warned her husband, "If we ever have a fire, you can leave everything else, but promise me you won't go out the door without my Bag of Life." She confessed her Bag of Life actually had grown into her Box of Life. When it became her Room of Life, she decided she couldn't risk a fire. She needed the File ... Don't Pile workshop.

Getting sidetracked is only part of the problem. The frustration also lies in the fact that paper usually isn't just confined to *one* closet. It's everywhere. Do you remember Nan, in Chapter One, the resource person for the neighborhood? Out of her desire to be of service to others by sharing ideas she had clipped and saved, she literally had covered every surface in her home. She reached her brink one dark, depressing day and telephoned me. It wasn't a problem of time any more. She was ready to block out a month, if necessary, to get her papers organized. It was a matter of *how.* "How do I begin?" she asked. What developed from that conversation is the Five-Step Preparation Plan. The plan changed her life and since has helped hundreds of people across the country as well. It is simple, and *it works!*

The Five-Step Preparation Plan

The Five-Step Preparation Plan is preliminary work. Just as it is necessary to prepare a room before it is painted, it is a wise investment of time to complete these preparatory steps before actually filing. You will need three groups of things: 1) three sheets of notebook paper and a pencil; 2) some cardboard boxes; 3) (optional) a soft drink. You might as well find a cozy niche and enjoy yourself!

Step 1. GENERALIZE
Your papers may be piled everywhere. Or your papers may be "filed" in a cabinet, and you want a better system. In either case, Step 1 in organizing your papers is to **determine what kinds of papers you have.** This is called the **Brainstorming Process.**

At the top of the first sheet of notepaper print these words:

BRAINSTORMING PAGE

Below these words, *jot a random list of the kinds of saveworthy papers that come into your life,* specifically, recipes, coupons, poems, and so forth. Think about what interests and activities you and others living with you have, and add them to the list *if* they involve paper. Don't get bogged down by order or neatness on the page. You are simply generalizing.

The purpose of the Brainstorming Page is to identify what kinds of papers you need to organize without physically spreading them out. Have you ever met anyone who must hold tangible objects before being able to describe them? He or she flits about fetching items saying, "Wait a minute. I'll just get it and show you." It can get very exhausting (for both of you) if there are many things to be described.

When I'm teaching a workshop, I rarely need to see the evidence, nor do you. Leave the stuff in the closet. All you need, at first, is a *generalized* list of the kinds of papers you want to organize. When Nan and I visited on her D-Day, we took the first step and brainstormed.

When you complete your Brainstorming Page, you are ready for Step 2.

Brainstorming Page

current bills
sales receipts
recipes!!
gardening
PTA
health records
birth certificates
poems, quotes
sewing
genealogy
maps, brochures
kid's school papers
craft ideas
decorating ideas
insurance papers
warranties/guarantees
needlepoint
tickets for Guthrie Theatre
magazine subscrip.
evening class registration
tax papers
Fluffy's records

hospital auxiliary
Women's Club
inspirational articles
diets/nutrition
Quilter's Assn.
calligraphy
Lion's Club
sailing
American Dental Assn.
photography
Nursing Class notes
resumes; job ideas
Book Club
camping info.
exercise/
beauty tips
child development
articles
tennis
golf

Step 2. CATEGORIZE

So that your filing project won't seem overwhelming, it's necessary next to hone down the list on the Brainstorming Page to a shorter one. Step 2 in organizing your papers is to **consolidate your subjects into broad categories.** This is the **Lumping Process.** It is one of the most important actions you'll take in organizing your papers. It involves a little concentration and time, but it pays off in the end.

At the top of the second sheet of notepaper, print these words:

BROAD CATEGORIES PAGE

First, scan the list you made on your Brainstorming Page. The papers will be one of two types — short-term or long-term. Short-term papers are the type that are pending. They require some kind of action and then can usually be thrown away. Long-term papers are the type that evoke either nostalgia or are handy to have for reference. They can and probably will be kept for years. On the Brainstorming Page, circle all the papers that are pending or short-term type papers such as theater tickets, current bills, evening class registration, and magazine subscriptions. Set aside these pending papers until Step 3.

Broad Categories Page

PERSONAL BUSINESS
sales receipts; tax papers;
birth certificates; insurance
health records; Fluffy's records;
warranties/guarantees

RELIGION
poems, quotes
inspirat. art.

COOKING
recipes; diets
nutrition

HOMEMAKING
gardening; needlepoint;
crafts; child developmt.;
sewing; decorating

TRAVEL
maps; camping
info; brochures

PERSONAL INTEREST/BARBARA
Women's Club; Hosp. Aux; Book Club; tennis
PTA; Quilter's Assn; calligraphy; exercise

PERSONAL INTEREST/BOB
Lion's Club; Am. Dental Assn.
photography; sailing:
golf

NURSING
class notes;
resumes;
job info.

JILL/BILL
school papers

GENEALOGY
reference and research

Group the remaining into large categories on the Broad Categories Page. This involves lumping similar subjects together under one broad heading such as **HOMEMAKING** or **COOKING** or **TRAVEL.**

Determining what category certain subjects can be filed in may be easier with some categories than others. Here are two suggestions:

1. Whether a category is broad sometimes depends on how much material is accumulated or can be potentially accumulated.

People often say, "I don't have much in this area, but if I had a good way of filing it, I know I'd save more." Other people already have a lot of papers concentrated in one area. One client asked me what I did with my sewing ideas and articles. I told her I kept them in a couple file folders in my **HOMEMAKING** category. She responded, "I've got so much, it probably wouldn't fit in a couple of *drawers!*" It was apparent that for her, **SEWING** is its own category.

If you have only a few papers on gardening or crafts, for example, include them as subjects within a broad category such as **HOMEMAKING.** If, however, you have a ton of stuff on gardening, make **GARDENING** a broad category. Subjects within this category might include: *Annuals, Biennials, Ferns, Hedges, Pruning,* and *Roses.* A **CRAFT** category might include: *Decoupage, Macrame, Origami, Quiet Books, Rock Art, Soft Boxes,* and *Woodcarving.*

The Appendix at the back of this book includes lists of suggested broad categories and subject headings.

2. Whether a category is broad sometimes depends on the purpose of the material accumulated.

Sometimes it isn't a matter of quantity in wanting to file certain papers separately. It's a matter of purpose. Perhaps you belong to a quliters association and you have materials concerning this organization. While you may have quilt ideas and patterns in a **HOMEMAKING** or in a **SEWING** category, you may not want to interfile organization newsletters with those materials. Papers such as these can be filed in a mini-category, for instance, **QUILTERS ASSOC.**

When you complete your Broad Categories Page — when your subjects are listed under their respective categories — you are ready for Step 3.

Step 3. CENTRALIZE/MINIMIZE

Think about the last time you washed the Thanksgiving dinner dishes. Did you do the dishes directly from the table one dish at a time? It would have taken all night, but it could have been possible. It's much more efficient if dishes are stacked first next to the sink. Paperwork isn't any different. Step 3 is organizing your papers is to **collect like papers together in one central location.** This is termed the **Gathering Process.**

At least two kinds of people are reading this book. There are the Obtrusive Clutterers, who have papers piled, without reservation, floor to ceiling, front door to back. Their key word is *on*. Papers can be found *on* cupboard counters, dining room tables, hutches, pianos, and stereos, *on* beds, chairs, desks, floors, and tops of refrigerators.

And there are the Elusive Clutterers, who may have just as much paper, but they keep it well hidden. Their key word is *in* (and sometimes *under*, as in under the bed and under the sofa). Papers can be found *in* cupboards, closets, basements, any furniture with drawers, the spare bedroom, and even in filing cabinets (piled, not filed).

Whether the paper is out in the open or well hidden, centralizing the papers is important. You'll probably find papers you've forgotten you had, find others you'll want to pitch, and perhaps find some duplicates. If you skip this step, you won't know what papers you actually do have on a subject.

If you are either kind of clutterer, here is a plan to help you gather or centralize your papers. It is

As Easy as ABC.
A. Get boxes.
Several cardboard boxes from the grocery store are needed to complete this step. The number of boxes depends on the amount of papers you have to organize, as well as the number of categories listed on your Broad Categories Page.
B. Label boxes.
You can use a felt-tip marking pen to label the boxes.
1. Print one category on a box, for example, **PERSONAL BUSINESS, NURSING,** or **WRITERS' GUILD.** You may have so much paper you may need three boxes just for **HOMEMAKING.**
2. Label one box **PENDING.** If you have difficulty keeping on top of papers that require action, put them in this box. Keep the box of "to do" papers in a location where it will be accessible. Chapter Eight discusses how to deal with pending papers.
3. Label one box **PROBLEMS.** When you begin sorting and you aren't sure in which category a paper should belong, it can be pitched temporarily into this box.

4. Label one box **TO BE CLIPPED.** When you're pitching and tossing, put all magazines or other materials to be clipped into this box. *Don't take the time in the midst of centralizing to clip articles from magazines.* You'll lose your momentum. It's better to gather together the papers you already have before creating more!
5. You may wish to label one box **SHARING.** Instead of throwing items you no longer want in the wastebasket, toss them into this box to share with others.

C. Fill boxes.
With the exception of the **PENDING** box, line up the labeled boxes in an area where they will be out of the way for a few days. Then, go from room to room and clean out your dressers, closets, under the beds, drawers in the kitchen, top of the refrigerator, under the sofa — anywhere and everywhere you have literally stashed papers. *Do one room at a time.* When you finish one room, go on to the next. You will begin to experience a real feeling of accomplishment.

Bring an armful of papers from each room to the area in which you have your boxes. Briefly examine each item. Determine the broad category in which it belongs. This goes fairly fast because the categories are obvious for many items. If you're stuck deciding on a category, put the paper in the **PROBLEMS** box. Some items may be difficult, especially if they are multicategorical. While you honestly want to save them, you don't want to rip them apart either. Eventually you'll have to face this box, but do the easy items first. After files are established, problems usually work themselves out.

Minimize the Mess.

As you centralize your papers, *minimize* them as well. Apply the "less is more" theory. Become an expert in "wastebasketry," as Edwin Bliss refers to it in his book, *Getting Things Done.* He says,

> [*Clutter*] hinders concentration on a single task, because your eye is constantly diverted by other things. Clutter can create tension and frustration, a feeling of being disorganized and "snowed under" . . . Insufficient use of the wastebasket leads to crowded files, a chaotic desk, . . . and a cluttered mind. Be ruthless in channeling paper into the wastebasket instead of into the files.

When discarding paper, fold it in half and put it in the wastebasket. Wadding paper into a crumpled ball is a waste of time and effort.

The ABC plan doesn't preclude, of course, the option of centralizing one category at a time. But you will sift through the same papers several times and waste time and energy.

A True Story.

On that dark, depressing day when Nan had descended to the pits, her way up and out from those piles of paper began with Steps 1 and 2. But the real ray of hope began to shine through when she completed Step 3. I spent two solid days working into the wee hours of the morning helping her centralize her papers. At the end of the second day, her husband was elated. There wasn't a piece of paper piled anywhere. They actually could eat on the kitchen table. Their beautiful home was restored. In the back bedroom, lined neatly along the wall, were her labeled boxes. Anyone who came into that room might have questioned her ability to locate papers in the five boxes on **RELIGION.** It would have been a slow process, but she knew basically where to look at that point. She had taken the most important steps in organizing her papers. She had *categorized* and *centralized* her paperwork. If she hadn't proceeded one step further, she was better off than she was before. She did continue getting organized, of course, and today is a new person. When you complete Step 3 you, too, can slide down the bannister to Step 4.

Step 4. PRIORITIZE

In a "Frank and Ernest" cartoon, the two principals were lounging on a park bench. One said to the other, "I'm going to re-evaluate my priorities someday, but there are a lot of other things I've got to do first." People inundated with paper often feel the same way. They look at the piles of stuff, sigh, "Where do I begin?" and give up. Step 4 in organizing your papers is to **list your broad categories in order of urgency for filing.** This is known as the **Evaluating Process.**

At the top of the third sheet of notepaper, print these words:

PRIORITIES LIST

Below these words, list in order of importance the categories or files you want to organize.

If you have had it with your recipes being in such a mess, write **COOKING** first on your Priorities List. If you're tired of having to sort through ten stacks of papers every time you need to find a price list for your Amway business, write **AMWAY** at the top of the list. If you have just assumed a leadership position in your women's group and your predecessor's method of filing was a shopping bag, you may need to make organizing those papers a high priority, write **RELIEF SOCIETY** at the top of the list.

```
O    Priorities List

     1. Homemaking
O    2. Cooking
     3. Personal Interest / Barbara
     4. Personal Interest / Bob
     5. Jill / Bill (each separate file)
     6. Nursing
     7. Religion
     8. Genealogy
     9. Travel
     10. Personal Business
O
```

You may have one category that has some semblance of order in which you are able to locate papers without too much difficulty. Although you're dissatisfied with that file and want it reorganized, put it low on the Priorities List. Begin the list with categories that are least organized. You can get by with a file that already has some order to it while you clean up the rest of the chaos.

One student said she listed her smallest category first. She wanted to be able to complete one file quickly so she could feel a sense of accomplishment.

If you have papers centralized in boxes, don't expect to have them all filed in one day. And don't feel guilty about it! You are getting started, and you will do it! The task will not be as overwhelming if you have a Priorities List. You'll need your Priorities List in Chapter Seven, so don't lose it. Before you ask, may I suggest a handy place to keep it is tacked inside the front cover of this book. We'll deal with it later after you learn the system.

When you complete your Priorities List, you are ready for Step 5, Organize!

Step 5. ORGANIZE

Step 5 in organizing your papers is to **file papers into folders in a box or drawer using the File ... Don't Pile system.** This is termed the **Filing Process.** In an attempt to organize their papers, many people don't consider Steps 1 through 4 and plunge right into Step 5. Unless the preliminary work is completed first, the **Filing Process** should not be started. Here's why.

Out of desperation many people load up on file folders believing that that's all there is to getting organized. Seeking a cure-all, they buy every adorable organizing gadget available at office supply and stationery stores. Filing cabinets are *not* the cure-all. The answer? It's the *system* that counts, not the equipment. Without the system, the filing cabinet becomes just another place to stash papers. As Don Fraser stated in *Record-Chronicle,* Denton, Texas, "The trouble with having a place for everything is how often it gets filled up with everything else." File drawers get filled with all sorts of things besides paper — yarn, toys, hammers, fishing gear, and so forth.

Don't get me wrong — filing cabinets are great. Get them if you can afford them. But if you can't, don't let that stop you from filing. It doesn't matter what you store your file folders in when using the File ... Don't Pile system. You'll be able to retrieve what you want when you need it. After many years of using apple and orange boxes covered with contact paper, I recently hit the "big time." It was a memorable day when I acquired my first real live metal filing cabinet.

Finding the Time To File

Completing Steps 1 through 4 can take as few as two or three days. It depends on how much paper you have piled and how much time you want to commit to the project. You'll be amazed how quickly files can be established. If you have been postponing getting your papers organized because you dreaded it as a monumental chore, what you need to do is to strike that fear. Filing is not that giant of a job. It will not take forever. It won't even take six months if you buckle down right now and make it a top priority. Block out some time, and make it your project. If time is a problem, follow the admonition of Abraham Lincoln: "Determine that the thing can and shall be done and then ... find the way." If you work full time, try what two of my students did. They reserved two weeks of weekday evenings to set up the system. Set a deadline when you want to have your papers organized. If it means having to put a big "X" on your calendar every Monday for a month so you won't schedule something else during your filing time, do it.

When your papers are categorized and centralized and you have prioritized which papers you want to organize first, you are ready to learn the Filing Process. The next four chapters explain how to file papers using the File ... Don't Pile system. Again, I encourage you to read the chapters in sequence. The system has two methods for filing papers. Chapter Four describes the A-Z METHOD. Chapter Five describes the PREFIX METHOD. Chapter Six discusses how to cross reference papers. Chapter Seven outlines a Plan of Attack to help you program your filing project and explains how to choose which of the two methods is best suited for the papers you want to file.

Summary
Five-Step Preparation Plan for Organizing Papers

Step 1. *Generalize*	Brainstorming Process
Step 2. *Categorize*	Lumping Process
Step 3. *Centralize/Minimize*	Gathering Process
Step 4. *Prioritize*	Evaluating Process
Step 5. *Organize*	Filing Process

Chapter Four

Get Your Feet Wet, Gerta!

Get Involved Instantly

Perhaps you know people who have their papers filed, but they are the only ones in their homes who know where to find anything. I have a rule in my house: You're welcome to anything in my files, but you get it yourself. I don't beat a path to the files whenever someone wants something. I doubt if you want to be a slave to your files either. The File ... Don't Pile system has been enthusiastically welcomed by so many because anyone can find materials quickly and easily without resorting to screaming, "Where did you put that paper about ...?"

This chapter examines one method of filing long-term papers, those papers that are kept for reference or reasons of nostalgia. This method, the A-Z METHOD, has saved countless footsteps.

One of the best ways to learn anything is to dive right in and get your feet wet. To introduce the A-Z METHOD, I'd like you to get involved instantly. It's as easy as 1-2-3.

1. Read the brief directions and sample problem describing how to use the A-Z METHOD.

2. Read the three demonstration questions.

3. "Look" in the hypothetical files to find the answers to the questions.

Brief Directions. On the next page is a sample drawer from a **CRAFT FILE** to illustrate how the A-Z METHOD works. Once you learn the technique, you'll be able to locate material in any category using this method.

1. The first file folder in the drawer is the **CRAFT FILE INDEX.**
   Remove the Index.

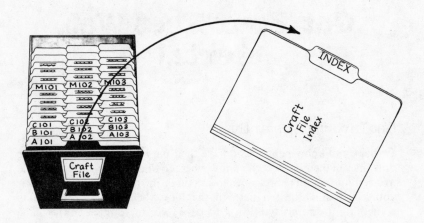

2. Let's assume you want a macrame pattern from this file.
   Since *Macrame* would be the logical subject and it begins with the letter "M," turn to the "M" page in the **CRAFT FILE INDEX.**
   Notice in the left-hand column of the "M" page that the code assigned to the subject *Macrame* is M103.

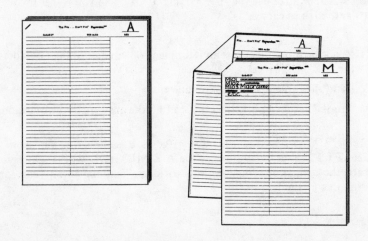

3. Retrieve the file folder marked M103 from the **CRAFT FILE** drawer. Information about *Macrame,* including patterns, is in this folder.

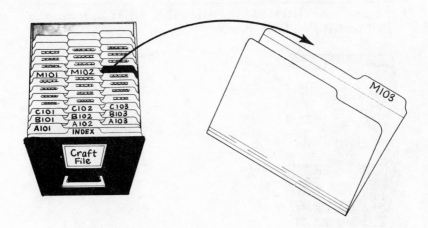

The code for *Macrame,* M103, is cited on each item filed in the M103 file folder for easy refiling.

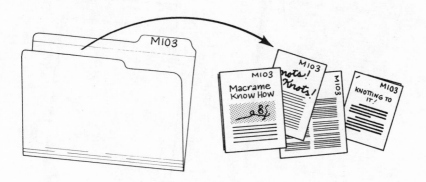

Now put yourself to the test by reading three demonstration questions and "look" in some hypothetical files for the answers.

> *Demonstration Question 1*
> *Category:* **HOMEMAKING**
> *I'm going to make a lamp out of this old bottle as soon as I find out where I put the directions.*

1. Remove the **HOMEMAKING FILE INDEX** from the **HOMEMAKING FILE** drawer.

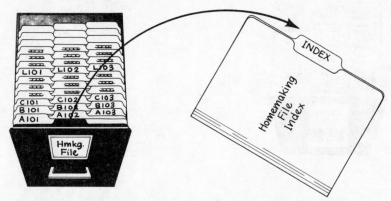

2. Because a lamp is the end product, *Lamps* is the likely subject under which to look in the Index. (In case other subjects might come to mind, for example, *Bottles,* cross referencing is the key. This is discussed in Chapter Six.)

    Since *Lamps* begins with the letter "L," turn to the "L" page in the **HOMEMAKING FILE INDEX.** Notice in the left-hand column of the "L" page that the code assigned to the subject *Lamps* is L101.

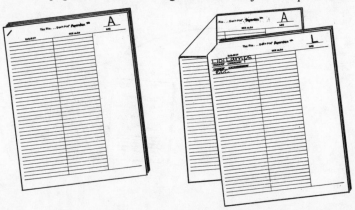

3. Retrieve the file folder marked L101 from the **HOMEMAKING FILE** drawer. Information about *Lamps,* including directions for making a lamp from old bottles, is in this folder.

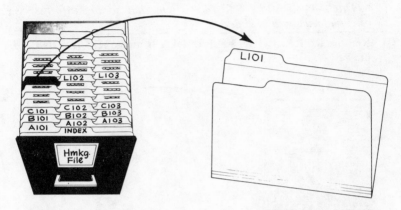

The code for *Lamps,* L101, is cited on each item filed in the L101 file folder for easy refiling.

Have you ever experienced a similar dilemma? You have an old bottle, but can't find the lamp directions. Or, you have the directions, but can't find the bottle? One woman in a workshop related that she had a bag of caramels and couldn't find the recipe in which she wanted to use them. By the time she found the recipe, the kids had eaten all the caramels!

Demonstration Question 2
Category: RELIGION
You are faced with a sudden death in the family. Where are those thoughtful poems and quotes that would comfort Uncle Fred? Where is the article that so beautifully explained death to children?

---

1. Remove the **RELIGION FILE INDEX** from the **RELIGION FILE** drawer.

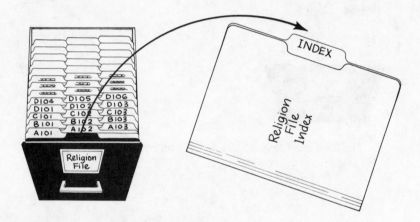

2. The logical subject to look under in in the Index would be *Death*.
   Since *Death* begins with the letter "D," turn to the "D" page in the **RELIGION FILE INDEX**.
   Notice in the left-hand column of the "D" page that the code assigned to the subject *Death* is D106.

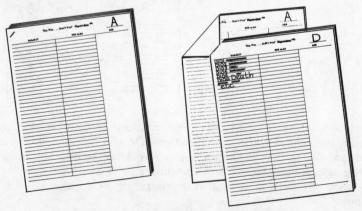

3. Retrieve the file folder marked D106 from the **RELIGION FILE** drawer.

Information about *Death*, including poems, quotes, and articles, is in this folder.

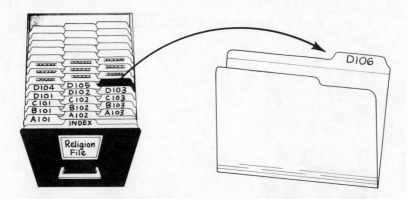

The code for *Death*, D106, is cited on each item filed in the D106 file folder for easy refiling.

Remember, categories usually are determined by what kind and how much material has been accumulated. Since I have only one folder with information on the subject of *Death*, it is filed in a logical category, **RELIGION**. One of my clients, however, has a whole drawer of materials on death that she uses in teaching death awareness classes. Therefore, for her filing needs, **DEATH** becomes a category broken down into specific subjects such as: *Cremation, Mourning, Sudden Infant Death Syndrome,* and *Suicide*.

> *Demonstration Question 3*
> *Category:* **COOKING**
> *Do you remember that yummy Mexican dish Gwynne Smith served at the fall luncheon — Indian Tacos? I think I'll fix that for dinner tonight.*

1. Remove the **COOKING FILE INDEX** from the **COOKING FILE** drawer.

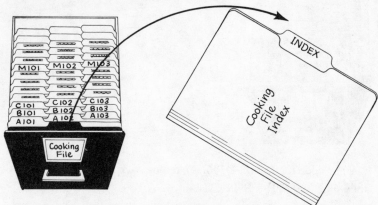

2. If you are really big on tacos and have enough recipes, it might warrant having one folder designated just for taco recipes. More likely, the Indian Taco recipe is filed under the subject *Mexican Dishes*.

   Since *Mexican Dishes* begins with the letter "M," turn to the "M" page in the **COOKING FILE INDEX.** Notice in the left-hand column of the "M" page that the code assigned to the subject *Mexican Dishes* is M102.

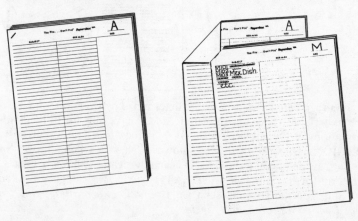

3. Retrieve the file folder marked M102 from the **COOKING FILE** drawer. Information about *Mexican Dishes,* including the recipe for Indian Tacos, is in this folder.

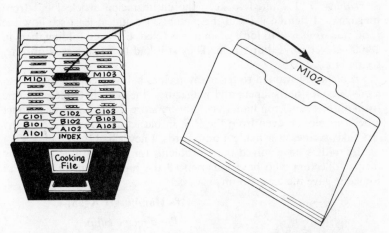

The code for *Mexican Dishes,* M102, is cited on each item filed in the M102 file folder for easy refiling.

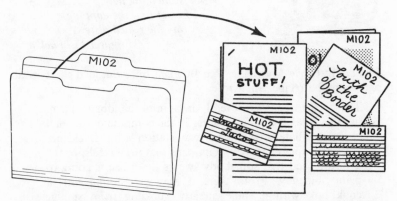

Before you feel threatened and clutch your 3″ x 5″-card recipe box you've had for a hundred years, don't panic. I'm not asking you to throw it out, nor am I saying a two-drawer file cabinet is a *must* in your kitchen. (In the first place, most kitchens wouldn't have room for a two-drawer file cabinet.)

Go ahead, ask — everyone else does. "Pat, do you *really* keep your recipes in file folders?" My answer, "Yes, I really do." I started with the traditional 3" x 5"-card recipe box. In a short time it graduated to a 4" x 6". Then I tried flip chart binders, notebooks, you name it. None of the methods on the market solved my two big recipe problems.

Problem 1. I wanted to keep the entire recipe article I cut from magazines. I figured if I had the pictures, I could at least see how the food was *supposed* to look when it was fixed. But even folding them in 18,000 clever ways didn't help. They still had to be squeezed into my recipe box.

Problem 2. I wanted to *try* many recipes before I copied them onto cards. Besides newspapers and magazines, the "try first" recipes came from dittoed luncheon handouts, grocery store flyers, backs of product labels, envelopes, even from the P.S. in old letters. Hardly any of my "try first" recipes ever made it onto cards. I never had the time!

File folders have solved these problems for me as well as for many recipe collectors who have experienced the predicament in this verse someone gave me in one of my classes:

It's Hamburger Again

I'm a recipe clipper
I pile them in drawers.
They're yellow with age And
I hoard them by scores;
But when I decide that I'll try
something new,
I can't find the clipping,
my file's such a stew.
                    Margaret Fishback

In *Family Circle* Magazine, Peg Bracken once outlined the typical progression of a recipe. She wrote:

> The recipe mellows several days in a handbag. Then, usually, it takes a long breather in the compote on the hall chest, or whatever the family way station is for drycleaner receipts, paper clips, ball-point pens that need refills, or the avocado seed that somebody swears he or she is going to plant someday. From there it may get stuffed into a cookbook with a spine already buckling from similar insertions. Or — and this is the real crossroads — it may go into a shoe box that's already the overflowing repository of the same kind of clippings. Once it gets into that shoe box, the prognosis, I'm afraid, is poor. Though you tell yourself that sorting recipes is good rainy-day therapy, so are many other things; and there seems to be a lot more recipes than rainy days.

Whether you have room in your kitchen for a two-drawer file or a small tote file box kept in the closet down the hall, file folders will save the day. If you wish, you can still keep your 3″ x 5″-card box with your favorite, more frequently used recipes. I've dispensed with mine and put the cards into the folders. I've realized over the years it's better having my recipes all centralized. There's a wonderful way to cross reference recipes from cookbooks, too, and this is discussed in Chapter Six.

A-Z METHOD

If there is a great deal of material to be filed in a given category or if the category has potential for growth (specifically, more than thirty-five file folders), I recommend the A-Z METHOD of filing.

Two major principles are used in the A-Z METHOD:

1. *The key to each category is the A-Z METHOD Paperdex.*™

2. *Subjects and tabs of file folders are assigned a code.*

Both principles are *always* used regardless of which category is being filed.

The Paperdex

Most filing systems have an index of some nature. I have dubbed the index used in the File . . . Don't Pile system the Paperdex. It is probably one of the fastest to set up and use. The purpose of the Paperdex is *to serve as a key place where codes assigned to subjects and any cross reference notes can be recorded.*

An A-Z METHOD Paperdex consists of twenty-four sheets of specially lined 8½″ x 11″ paper. One set of twenty-four sheets is needed for each broad category using the A-Z METHOD. To obtain preprinted A-Z METHOD Paperdexes use the order form at the back of this book.

Each page of the A-Z METHOD Paperdex represents one letter of the alphabet except the last page which includes the letters, "x-y-z." A fine-tip marking pen can be used to print the letter on the short line in the upper right-hand corner of each page.

There are three columns on each page of the A-Z METHOD Paperdex. The left-hand column is the **SUBJECT,** the center column is the **SEE ALSO,** and the far right-hand column is the **SEE.** Each column will be discussed separately. This chapter explains how to use the **SUBJECT** column. Chapter Six describes the **SEE ALSO** and **SEE** columns which are used in cross referencing.

The A-Z METHOD Paperdex is filed in its own folder and is kept at the beginning of the category in the drawer. A colored folder is preferable to manila because color not only makes it easier to locate the index, but it also serves as a divider between categories if more than one is filed in the same drawer.

Below is a partial page from an A-Z METHOD Paperdex for a **RELIGION FILE:**

The File ... Don't Pile" Paper Index©		S
SUBJECT	SEE ALSO	SEE
S101 — Savior	C110;	Sunday -S106
S102— Stewardship		Sorrow - D106
S103— Sacrifice		Sadness- D105
S104— Sincerity		Steadfastness-
S105— Scriptures	B101; N102;O103	E101
S106— Sabbath		Swearing—P104
S107— Sacrament		
S108— Service	C105	
S109— Sin		
S110 — Satan		

Advantages of the Paperdex. Are there any advantages to using a Paperdex instead of a card index? On a whim, after using the Paperdex for several years, I experimented to see if 3" x 5" cards would be a better method of indexing. Let me save you a lot of time and trouble and tell you the difference.

The first difference I learned was how much more time and work it was to keep a card index up-to-date.

It may be a bent in my personality or the librarian in me, but I lean toward cards in an index file that are typewritten, not handwritten. That might be because my own handwriting is never the same from one day to the next, or perhaps because I can never find the same pen two days in a row. Handwritten cards can become a montage of colors and styles, too soon legible, too soon not.

After several days of typing subject and cross reference cards, my experiment didn't seem much like a whimsical project — more like a monster that owned me. When I finished, the stack of cards needed to be arranged in a box in alphabetical order. Thereafter, whenever I filed a new subject, I was obligated to trot to the typewriter to type the necessary cards. That was shortlived. I began making lists to save time, so I could type a bunch of cards at once. I ended up not knowing what papers were filed because some subjects were typed on index cards and some were on the "to be typed" lists. Like my ironing, I never could get caught up. Instead of one, I had created two files to maintain — a file of papers in folders and a file of cards for my file of papers.

The second difference I learned was a card index can be very hard on one's back. The ultimate happened. I accidentally knocked the card index onto the floor. Because I didn't have the kind of box with a rod in it, the cards flew everywhere. Nothing could have made me happier. I chucked the experiment and hugged my Paperdex.

It probably takes sixty seconds to pencil in a new subject and the related cross references in a A-Z METHOD Paperdex. (So much for trips to the typewriter.) And you never have to hunt for blank cards. (One A-Z METHOD Paperdex for a category will last for years.)

There are other advantages of using A-Z METHOD Paperdex besides time, convenience, and money. These advantages will surface as you read and learn more about the File ... Don't Pile system and as you use it.

The Code

The code in the A-Z METHOD consists of two parts — a letter and a number.

The Letter. The letter in the code **is determined by the first letter of the subject** under which an item is filed. All subjects beginning with the letter "A" begin with an "A" in their codes, "B" subjects with "B," and so forth. For example:

A101 *Arizona*   M101 *Mexico*

A102 *Athens*   M102 *Maine*

A103 *Africa*   M103 *Miami*

Subject headings do not need to be limited to one word. In a **COOKING FILE INDEX,** I saw this entry: F104 *Food Gift Ideas* and in a **HOMEMAKING FILE INDEX,** A107 *Activities for Kids.* The letter in the code is determined by the first letter of the first word of the subject.

The Number. The number in the code **is simply determined by the order in which an item is removed from a box to be coded.**

To illustrate how subjects are assigned code letters and numbers, let's organize a hypothetical **TRAVEL FILE.** Maps, brochures, articles, and so forth, are all centralized in one big box. The A-Z METHOD Paperdex is lettered appropriately in the upper right-hand corner of each page. Everything appears to be all systems go. Before anything is taken out of the box, answer this question. *Are the papers going to be conveniently alphabetized as they were gathered and stuffed into this box?* Not likely. Brochures about Arizona aren't necessarily going to be the first items on the top of the heap and Zanzibar isn't going to float to the bottom. Don't worry about it. It doesn't make any difference.

Let's remove the first three papers from the box. Perhaps the first item is a brochure about Mexico. Since *Mexico* is the logical subject to look under when this brochure is needed, the letter assigned in the code is "M." Because *Mexico* is the first "M" subject to be filed, the number assigned in the code is 101, or 1. (I prefer the longer number because the code seems easier to read.) The code for *Mexico,* therefore, is M101, or M-1. Thereafter, any time information about *Mexico* is filed, it is coded M101 or M-1.

Remove the next item from the box. It is an article about traveling in England. The letter assigned in the code for the subject, *England,* is "E." Because England is the first "E" subject filed, the number assigned in the code is 101, or 1. The code for *England,* therefore, is E101, or E-1. Thereafter, any time information about *England* is filed, it is coded E101 or E-1.

Remove the third item from the box. It is a map of Maine. The letter assigned in the code for the subject, *Maine,* is "M." Because *Maine* is the second "M" subject to be filed, the number assigned in the code is 102, or 2. Remember, M101 has already been assigned to the subject *Mexico* so the *next available number* on the "M" page, M102, is used for the subject *Maine.* The code for Maine, therefore, is M102, or M-2. Thereafter, any time information about *Maine* is filed, it is coded M102 or M-2.

As the box of travel papers empties, more coded subjects, or "pigeonholes," are established in which to file materials. The "pigeonholes" are easily identified by their codes — for example, C101 is *Canada;* C102 is *California;* G109 is *Germany;* S106 is *Switzerland.* If there isn't enough material on Vermont, New Hampshire, Maine, and Massachusetts to warrant separate file folders for each subject, put the papers into one folder, assign it the subject, *New England States,* and code it N105, for example. Similarly, there might only be one piece of paper about a city or a place, for instance, Bangor, Maine, or Hearst Castle. Instead of filing only one piece of paper in a folder, interfile the paper in the most logical subject — i.e., Bangor, Maine, could be filed within the subject *Maine,* and Hearst Castle could be filed within the subject, *California.* The information can be cross referenced as directed in Chapter Six.

Now that you know what the A-Z METHOD Paperdex and code are, let's apply these principles using the brochure about Mexico as an example. Follow the three steps as outlined to transfer the brochure from the messy box into a file folder in the **TRAVEL FILE.**

Determine the code and subject of the brochure, specifically, M101 *Mexico.* (Assume that *Mexico* is the first subject to be listed on the "M" page of the **TRAVEL FILE INDEX.)** Next, follow these three steps:

Step 1. MARK THE INDEX.

> *IN PENCIL,* print the assigned code — M101 — and the subject — *Mexico* — in the subject column on the "M" page in the **TRAVEL FILE INDEX.** *It is important to record the code and the subject in the Paperdex, because it is the key to finding in which folder the information is filed.*

The File . . . Don't Pile" Paperdex ™

SUBJECT	SEE ALSO	SEE
M101 – Mexico		

M

Print the code first, then the subject in the left-hand column. **Always enter codes and subjects in pencil** in the Paperdex. There are advantages to using pencil, which I'll share later.

Subjects will not appear in alphabetical order in the subject column. It isn't necessary. The column can be scanned at a glance.

Step 2. MARK THE ITEM.
Print the assigned code — M101 — in the upper right-hand corner of the brochure about Mexico. *It is important to mark the code on each item so it can be easily refiled after it is used.* The code can be printed in pencil on the back of the item if desired. Some

papers, if shared with others, might not appear too aesthetic with a code splashed across the top.

Step 3. MARK THE FILE FOLDER.
USE A WIDE-TIP FELT PEN to mark the codes on the tabs of file folders. The code is easier to read if a wide-tip, rather than a fine-tip, pen is used. Select a different colored pen for each broad category — for example, **COOKING** - red; **TRAVEL** - brown; **RELIGION** - blue.

Another way to color-code categories is to use different colored file folders. This is pretty, but also more expensive. Instead, use only one colored file folder for the Paperdex. A color-coordinated felt-tip pen can be used to mark the tabs of plain manila file folders for the category.

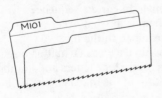

Print the assigned code — M101 — on a **LEFT**-tabbed file folder. The tabs of the folders are filed in a left to right sequence. A left tab is needed for the number 101 since it is the first number for the letter "M" to be filed.

In the A-Z METHOD,
always start each new letter with a left tab.
It keeps the tabs in the proper sequence.

Naturally, when first beginning, a lot of left-tabbed file folders will be used. Several left tabs may follow one after another. Some letters may be missing but don't be alarmed. See the example on the left. The file will fill in as additions are made. See the example on the right.

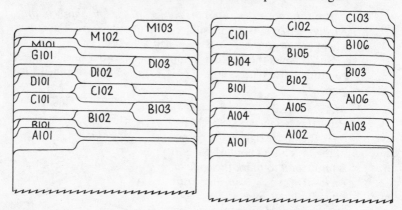

Remember, the file folders in the A-Z METHOD will never be out of sequence as long as *each new letter is started with a left tab.*

Advantages of the code. Someone asked me why I didn't simply write the subject, for example, *Mexico* or *Souffles,* on the tab of the file folder and be done with it. Why bother with codes? That's a fair question. Here is the answer.

If subjects are written on tabs of file folders, the folders must be filed in alphabetical order. If they are not in alphabetical order, it is chaos locating a particular subject. What happens to the tab positions on the folders when the subjects are alphabetized? That's right, the tabs never remain in sequence. Each time a new subject is added the order is thrown off. One of the biggest advantages of printing codes instead of subjects on tabs is that it eliminates the need to alphabetize the file folders within each letter.

Because tabs are coded,
the folders always remain in correct sequence
no matter how often or in what order
new subjects are added to the file.

Another advantage of coding is that it doesn't matter how well or how poorly you write. Anyone can print block letters and numbers, and that is all that is necessary to label tabs of file folders. Which file drawer do you think is easier to read?

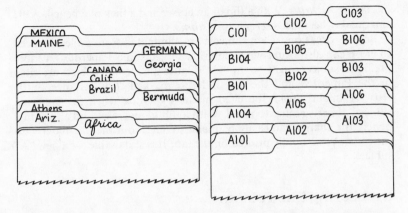

Coding also saves time and money. You might decide to no longer save material on a certain subject. Let's say an interest in antiques or motorcycles wanes; or the doctor says cut out all cheese; or a move into an apartment means there is no longer a place to garden. What happens to the file folder after the papers are pitched? If the file folder is in good condition, it can be used for another subject. But if a subject is written on the tab, these are the alternatives: Scribble out the old subject, and write a new subject above it; buy labels to glue over the top of the old subject; or fold the file folder over and use the back of the tab (unless another subject is already written on that side, too).

This dilemma is never experienced when codes are used on the tabs. If the papers on *Arthritis* are discarded from a **HEALTH FILE,** the A102 file folder is fine for a new "A" subject. There are no labels to buy, no folders to reshuffle to keep order, no words to scribble out. And that leads us to the pencil.

But ... Why Pencil?

Crossword puzzles can be done in permanent ink at the Optimists Club, but when subjects are entered in the Paperdex remember the rule: **Always work in pencil in the Paperdex.** Here's why.

When librarians decide to discard titles from a collection, it involves more than just pulling the books off from the shelves. Without also removing the cards for those titles in the card catalog, library patrons cannot know which books are no longer available.

If the subject *Arthritis* is removed from the **HEALTH FILE,** as is the case above, it isn't just a matter of dumping the paper from the file folder into the wastebasket. The file folder might be empty, but according to the index, A102 still contains information about *Arthritis.* Since subjects in the Paperdex are written in pencil, it's simply a matter of erasing *Arthritis*. With a flip of an eraser and a flick of a pencil, A102 can quickly become *Allergies* or *Asthma*.

Besides occasions when subjects are eliminated from a file, the need to erase can also occur when entering subjects in a Paperdex. A more preferred subject might be thought of after a code and subject are cited in the Paperdex and the file folder is marked. For instance, A105 *Anxiety* might already be cited in the Paperdex when the preferred subject, *Worry*, comes to mind. With a flip of an eraser and a flick of a pencil, the change can easily be made. What about the file folder with the code, A105, boldly printed on the tab? It is still usable for a new "A" subject.

Numbering The Folders

One morning Jennie Lin Strong, a workshop participant, telephoned me. She said she had a great inspiration while organizing her **COOKING FILE.** I thought she had created a new dish. She hadn't — but she did create a wonderful timesaver. I appreciate it, and so have many others.

She said when she assigned a code to a subject, let's say, S115 *Salads*, she either had to look in her file drawer or count out which tab position — left, center, or right — was needed in order to mark her file folder. So, she created the Reference Chart idea. There are two examples at the end of this chapter. One chart is designed for use with third-cut tabbed folders, the other chart is for use with fifth-cut. The tabs of the folders are staggered in three positions for third-cut and in five positions for fifth-cut. The Reference Chart for Numbering Third-Cut Tabs makes it easy to determine which tab position is needed. For example, S115 *Salads* uses a right tab.

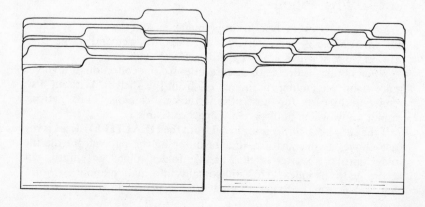

REFERENCE CHART FOR NUMBERING
THIRD-CUT TABS

Left Tab	Center Tab	Right Tab
101	102	103
104	105	106
107	108	109
110	111	112
113	114	115
116	117	118
119	120	121
122	123	124
125	126	127
128	129	130
131	132	133
134	135	136
137	138	139
140	141	142
143	144	145

REFERENCE CHART FOR NUMBERING
FIFTH-CUT TABS

Left Tab	Second Tab	Center Tab	Fourth Tab	Right Tab
101	102	103	104	105
106	107	108	109	110
111	112	113	114	115
116	117	118	119	120
121	122	123	124	125
126	127	128	129	130
131	132	133	134	135
136	137	138	139	140
141	142	143	144	145

Summary
Two Principles of the A-Z METHOD

Principle 1. *The key to each category is the A-Z METHOD Paperdex.*

    a. It serves as a key place where codes and subjects and any cross reference notes can be recorded.

    b. It consists of twenty-four sheets of specially lined 8½" x 11" paper. Each pages represents one letter of the alphabet, except the last page which represents "x-y-z."

Principle 2. *Subjects and tabs of file folders are assigned a code.*

Three Steps for Filing Papers
Using A-Z METHOD

Step 1. *Mark the index.*
Always enter codes and subjects in the index in pencil.

Step 2. *Mark the item.*
Always mark code on each item so it can be easily refiled.

Step 3. *Mark the file folder.*
Always start each new letter with a left tab to keep tabs in proper sequence.

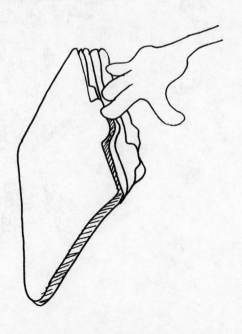

Chapter Five
Adapting the System

Get Involved Instantly

Some people inundated with paper regard the idea of filing with the same reluctance they do the idea of cleaning their ovens. They know the chore needs to be done, but they keep postponing it either because there are more exciting things to do or because the job seems so overwhelming they don't want to begin. When the grime and grease reaches the smoke-alarm stage, they are compelled to take action.

Piles of paper reach a zenith, too. The File ... Don't Pile system is so simple and flexible, however, it doesn't matter what kinds of paper you have or how much paper you accumulate. Filing doesn't have to be a major production.

The nineteenth-century German writer Heinrich Heine, wrote: "The weathercock on the church spire, though made of iron, would soon be broken by the storm-wind, if it ... did not understand the noble art of turning to every wind." Like the weathercock, the two principles of the File ... Don't Pile system — 1) the Paperdex and 2) the code — stand firmly. The *way* in which these principles are adapted, however, is flexible. To assume the A-Z METHOD is the only way to file the diversity of papers people accumulate would be impractical. Not only do papers vary from one person to the next, but people also *change* individually. As interests and needs alter, the trails of paper in their lives reflect these differences.

While it's important to be flexible, it's equally important to maintain simplicity. Heine also said, "If the Romans had been obliged to learn Latin, they would have never conquered the world." The File ... Don't Pile system provides a simple alternative approach for filing when the A-Z METHOD doesn't apply to the kind and amount of papers to be organized. This chapter discusses the second method, the PREFIX METHOD.

Just as the A-Z METHOD was introduced in Chapter Four, the fastest way to become acquainted with the PREFIX METHOD is instant involvement. The following examples demonstrate that it, too, is as easy as 1 - 2 - 3.

1. Read the brief directions on how to use the PREFIX METHOD.

2. Read the two demonstration questions.

3. "Look" in the files to find the answers to the questions.

Brief Directions. Below is a sample drawer containing three small categories or mini-files to illustrate how the PREFIX METHOD works. The three mini-files are first, a **GAME FILE,** second, a **GIRL SCOUT FILE** and third, a **MONEY MANAGEMENT FILE.** Each mini-file or category in this drawer has its own Paperdex. Once you learn the technique, you'll be able to locate material in any category using this method.

1. The first file folder in this drawer is the **GAME FILE INDEX.** Remove the index.

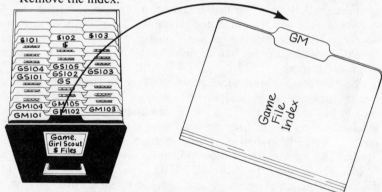

2. The Paperdex used in the PREFIX METHOD consists of only *one* sheet of paper, not twenty-four sheets as used in the A-Z METHOD.

The code used in the PREFIX METHOD begins with assigned prefix letters designating the category. In this case, GM represents **GAME.**

Let's assume you want a game idea to help your guests meet each other at your next party. Since *Icebreakers* would be a logical subject, this is the subject you need to look for in the **GAME FILE INDEX.** The subject heading, *Getting Acquainted,* could also be used. Choose the term you feel most comfortable using.

Notice in the left-hand column of the Paperdex that the code assigned to the subject *Icebreakers* is GM103.

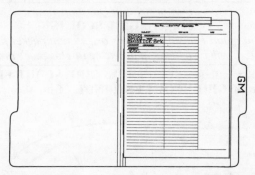

3. Retrieve the file folder marked GM103 from the **GAME FILE** in the drawer. Icebreaker games will be included in this folder.

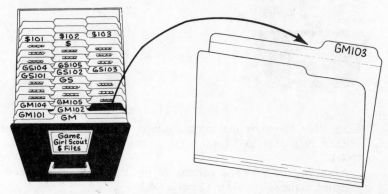

The code for *Icebreakers,* GM103, is cited on each item filed in the GM103 file folder for easy refiling.

Now put yourself to the test by reading two demonstration questions and "look" in some hypothetical files for the answers.

Demonstration Question 1
Category: **GIRL SCOUTS**
I'm sure glad I saved last year's orientation packet for Day Camp. It will be a big help in setting up this year's program.

---

1. The prefix letters assigned for the **GIRL SCOUT FILE** are GS. Remove the **GIRL SCOUT FILE INDEX** from the drawer.

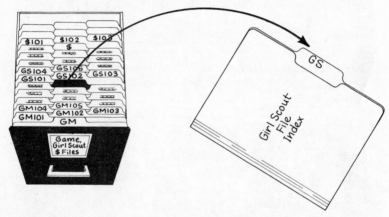

2. Since *Day Camp* is the logical subject in which to locate the orientation packet, look for this subject in the **GIRL SCOUT FILE INDEX.**

   Notice in the left-hand column of the Paperdex that the code assigned to the subject *Day Camp* is GS104.

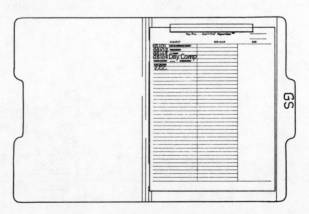

3. Retrieve the file folder marked GS104 from the **GIRL SCOUT FILE** in the drawer. Information about *Day Camp,* including the orientation packet, will be in this folder.

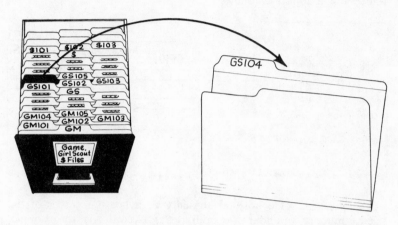

The code for *Day Camp,* GS104, is cited on each item filed in the GS104 file folder for easy refiling.

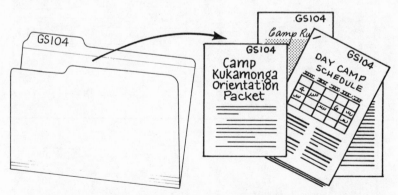

Membership in clubs and organizations automatically means paper in our lives, especially if positions of leadership are held. When someone telephones concerning Day Camp, the Girl Scout leader in the above example doesn't have to plow through one or two bulging file folders labeled *Girl Scout Stuff* to locate the needed information. Instead, she calmly goes to her **GIRL SCOUT FILE** and retrieves GS104.

Prefix letters can be adapted to fit any category. A leader in Camp Fire, for example, has similar materials to the Girl Scouts. To establish a **CAMP FIRE FILE,** the prefix letters, CF, can be used to designate the category. The **CAMP FIRE FILE INDEX** and corresponding file folders might appear as follows:

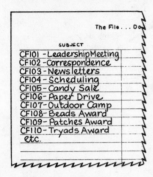
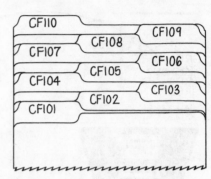

The president of a hospital auxiliary or a board member of the science museum can adapt the prefix letters accordingly, for example, **AUX** for **HOSPITAL AUXILIARY** and SM for **SCIENCE MUSEUM.** The Paperdex and tabs for each may appear as follows:

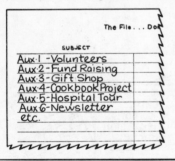
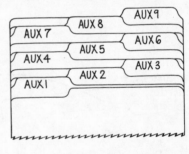

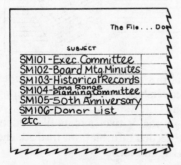
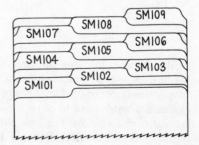

If the entire family is involved in a number of organizations and clubs, papers such as newsletters, directories, schedules, announcement flyers, and so forth, accumulate fast. The prefix letters, GRP, could be used to establish a **GROUPS FILE.**

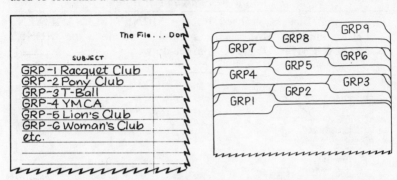

The File . . . Dor

SUBJECT
GRP-1 Racquet Club
GRP-2 Pony Club
GRP-3 T-Ball
GRP-4 YMCA
GRP-5 Lion's Club
GRP-6 Woman's Club
etc.

GRP9
GRP8
GRP7
GRP5
GRP6
GRP4
GRP2
GRP3
GRP1

If involvement in an organization increases, paperwork usually increases. Rather than cram papers all into one folder, assign two or three file folders in the **GROUPS FILE** to one organization, specifically, three folders for *Woman's Club,* and use subheadings:

GRP 6 - *Woman's Club - General Information*
GRP 7 - *Woman's Club - Education Committee*
GRP 8 - *Woman's Club - Spring Conference*

It might be necessary to delete a subject from the **GROUPS FILE,** if papers in that area increase greatly. The subject, *Pony Club,* for instance, might develop into its own category or mini-file. The prefix letter for the category **PONY CLUB** could be PC and a breakdown of subjects as follows:

PC101 - *Membership Drive*
PC102 - *Newsletters*
PC103 - *Pony Camp*
PC104 - *Riding Clinic*
PC105 - *Weekend Shows*

If you don't belong to many organizations, yet have a few papers of this nature to file, one option is to include them in a category such as **PERSONAL INTERESTS.** This category is general enough to include papers not only for organizations, but hobbies and other areas of personal interest, as well.

Keep in mind that the PREFIX METHOD is used for smaller categories or mini-files. If your hobby is photography and you have a truckload of papers involving this interest, use the A-Z METHOD to file those papers.

Demonstration Question 2
Category: **MONEY MANAGEMENT**
*Where is that information on when
to find the best bargains in stores?*

---

1. The prefix letters assigned for the **MONEY MANAGEMENT FILE** could be MM or the symbol $. Remove the **MONEY MANAGEMENT INDEX** from the drawer.

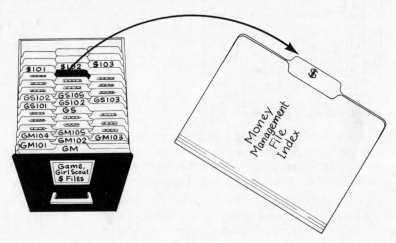

2. Since *Bargains* is the logical subject in which to locate the information, look for this subject in the **MONEY MANAGEMENT INDEX.**

   Notice in the left-hand column of the Paperdex that the code assigned to the subject, *Bargains,* is $102.

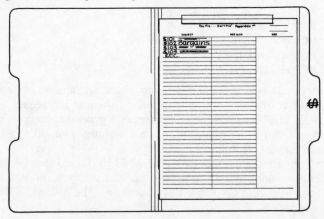

3. Retrieve the file folder marked $102 from the **MONEY MANAGE-MENT FILE** in the drawer.

 Information about *Bargains,* including articles and handouts, will be in this folder.

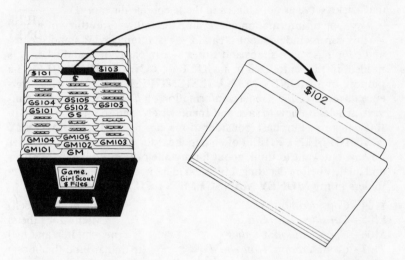

 The code for *Bargains,* $102, is cited on each item filed in the $102 file folder for easy refiling.

Many people clip and save money management information from magazines and newspapers. The articles usually wind up being stacked with the bills to be paid or interfiled with insurance policies and investment papers because the information is related. More frequently, the articles serve as bookmarks in the telephone directory.

Any type of information concerning the inflow or outflow of money — this can include coupons, catalogs, restaurant reviews and menus, and clippings about shops and stores — can easily be found when it is needed, if it is centralized in a **MONEY MANAGEMENT FILE**. The purpose of a **MONEY MANAGEMENT FILE** is to serve as a reference or resource file. General information on *how to* budget, *how to* invest, articles on *how to* save and spend wisely, and so forth, are filed in this category. Purchase considerations can be filed in the **MONEY MANAGEMENT FILE**. I often clip ideas for items I want to consider buying, but want to think about for a while or want to compare prices and quality before deciding. I file such ideas in one of four consideration folders in my **MONEY MANAGEMENT FILE**, specifically.

$104 - *Consideration/Me*	(items for myself)
$105 - *Consideration/Gift*	(items for others)
$106 - *Consideration/Clothes*	(my children and me)
$107 - *Consideration/Household*	(in and around the house)

A **MONEY MANAGEMENT FILE** does *not* include actual receipts, personal investments or copies of documents. Personally related papers of this nature are filed in a **PERSONAL BUSINESS FILE,** which is discussed in Chapter Nine.

PREFIX METHOD

If there isn't enough material to warrant the use of a separate sheet of paper for each letter of the alphabet in a Paperdex, i.e., the A-Z METHOD, treat the materials as a small category or mini-file. For this, I recommend using the PREFIX METHOD. This method of filing is especially effective for categories in which there are or expect to be thirty-five or fewer file folders. Like the A-Z METHOD, the PREFIX METHOD also uses the two major principles of the File ... Don't Pile system:

Principle 1. *The key to each category is the PREFIX METHOD Paperdex.*

Principle 2. *Subjects and tabs of file folders are assigned a code.*

These two principles are *always* used regardless which category is being filed. The *way* in which materials are coded, however, can be varied and adapted to suit individual needs.

The Paperdex

The purpose of the PREFIX METHOD Paperdex is the same as the A-Z METHOD. The Paperdex *serves as a key place where codes are assigned to subjects and cross reference notes can be recorded.* A PREFIX METHOD Paperdex sheet is needed for each category using the PREFIX METHOD.

There are two short lines in the upper right-hand corner of the PREFIX METHOD Paperdex. On the top line, print the prefix letters assigned to represent the category. On the bottom line, print the name of the category.

The PREFIX METHOD Paperdex page is divided into three columns. The left-hand column is the **SUBJECT,** the center column is the **SEE ALSO** and the far right-hand column is the **SEE.** Each column will be discussed separately. This chapter explains how to use the **SUBJECT** column. Chapter Six describes the **SEE ALSO** and **SEE** columns which are used in cross referencing.

The PREFIX METHOD Paperdex is kept in a folder at the beginning of the category in the drawer. A colored folder is preferable to manila because color not only makes it easier to locate the index, but it also serves as a divider between categories if more than one is filed in the same drawer.

Below is a partial page from a PREFIX METHOD Paperdex for a **SMALL BUSINESS FILE.**

The File... Don't Pile™ Paperdex™		SB — Small Business
SUBJECT	**SEE ALSO**	**SEE**
SB101 - General Info. Articles		Filing business
SB102 - Classes to take/Wkshp		name - SB105
SB103 - Record keeping		All the Good Old
SB104 - Taxes		Girls - SB108
SB105 - Legal Information		Accounting - SB103
SB106 - Market/Advertis.		
SB107 - Insurance		
SB108 - Networking		
SB109 - Financing		
SB110 - Franchises		
etc.		

A **SMALL BUSINESS FILE** is a reservoir of reference information for a person preparing to go into business or who owns a small business. General articles and pamphlets on *how to* start a business, *how to* advertise, financial information, and so forth, are filed in a **SMALL BUSINESS FILE.** On the other hand, actual receipts, copies of documents, information specifically concerning a company are filed in a category for that business, i.e., **FISHER ENTERPRISES, INC. FILE.**

The Code

The code in the PREFIX METHOD consists of two parts — prefix letters and a number.

The Prefix Letters. The prefix letters in the code **are determined by the first (or first few) letters of the** *category.* There are generally no more than two or three prefix letters in a code. The prefix is not an acronymn, although it can be. Some examples of prefix letters might be:

PB - **PERSONAL BUSINESS**
RC - **RED CROSS**
WFC - **WOMEN'S FACULTY CLUB**
SAT - **SINGLES ALL TOGETHER**

Unlike the A-Z METHOD in which the letter in the code changes according to the first letter of each subject, *the prefix letters in the code in the PREFIX METHOD remain constant.*

The Number. The number in the code is **determined either by the order in which an item is removed from the box to be coded or by the predetermined order the subjects are sequenced.**

It is possible before filing papers in the PREFIX METHOD to first arrange the subjects in a specific sequence. Code numbers are then assigned in corresponding order.

For instance, a teacher may file materials according to the sequence lessons are taught. A nutrition series of ten lessons may be filed:

NT101 - *Introduction*
NT102 - *Breads/Cereals/Sugars/Fats*
NT103 - *Protein 1 - Meat*
NT104 - *Protein 2 - Nuts, etc.*
NT105 - *Vitamins and Minerals*
NT106 - *Fruits and Vegetables*
NT107 - *Milk Products*
NT108 - *Water*
NT109 - *Expectant Mothers*
NT110 - *Babies and Children*

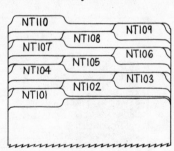

A mini **TRAVEL FILE** may be sequenced geographically:

TR101 - *U.S./Eastern*
TR102 - *U.S./Central*
TR103 - *U.S./Mountain*
TR104 - *U.S./Pacific*
TR105 - *Canada*
TR106 - *Mexico*
TR107 - *Central/South America*
TR108 - *Europe*

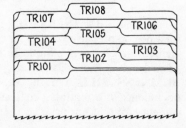

A researcher or student can file papers in a chronological sequence in an
ENGLISH LITERATURE FILE:

EL101 - *Anglo-Saxon Period*
EL102 - *Norman-French Period*
EL103 - *Age of Chaucer*
EL104 - *Renaissance/Nondramatic*
EL105 - *Renaissance/Dramatic*
EL106 - *Renaissance/Shakespeare*
EL107 - *Classicism*
EL108 - *Romanticism*
EL109 - *Victorian*
EL110 - *20th Century*

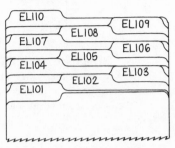

Information can be sequenced according to the order of importance
to the filer. Simply ask, "What papers do I need access to first, second,
and so forth?" As a board member for a woman's organization, I've
arranged materials in the order of their significance as well as
accessibility:

VT101 - *Statistics/Percentage Charts*
VT102 - *Directories/Calendar*
VT103 - *Stake Board Notes*
VT104 - *Goals and Assignments*
VT105 - *Ward Supervisors*
VT106 - *Stake Leadership Meeting*
VT107 - *Ward Visiting Teachers*
VT108 - *Visiting Teacher Convention*
VT109 - *Motivational Ideas*
VT110 - *Compassionate Service*

Now that you know what the PREFIX METHOD Paperdex and
code are, let's apply these principles using a **NUTRITION FILE** and a
pamphlet, "The Great Vitamin Mystery," as an example. To file the
pamphlet, follow the same three steps outlined in the A-Z METHOD in
Chapter Four.

Step 1. MARK THE INDEX.
   IN PENCIL, print the assigned code — NT105 — and the
   subject — *Vitamins* — in the subject column in the **NUTRI-
   TION FILE INDEX.** *It is important to record the code and the
   subject in the Paperdex because it is the key to finding in which
   folder information is filed.*

Print the code first, then the subject in the left-hand column. **Always enter codes and subjects in pencil.** Subjects are not arranged in alphabetical order. It isn't necessary. The column can be scanned at a glance.

Step 2.   *MARK THE ITEM.*
Print the assigned code — NT105 — in the upper right-hand corner of the pamphlet on vitamins. *It is important to mark the code on each item so it can be easily refiled after it is used.* The code can be printed in pencil on the back of the item if desired.

Step 3.   *MARK THE FILE FOLDER.*
USE A WIDE-TIP FELT PEN to mark the codes on the tabs of file folders. The code is easier to read if a wide-tip, rather than a fine-tip, pen is used. Select a different colored pen for each category and color-coordinate the file folder used for the Paperdex. Colors are bound to repeat themselves if there are many categories, but the prefix letters will serve to distinguish. For instance, GS, $, and AUX can all be coded in green, but the three categories should not be stored in the same drawer. If only one drawer is available, assign each category a different color.

The tabs of the file folders are filed in a left to right sequence, as in the A-Z METHOD. *Use a left tab for the first number and continue the left-center-right sequence consecutively.* The prefix letters remain constant so the first number starts the sequence. As each new subject is added, it is assigned the next available number and the next tab in sequence.

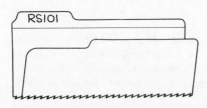

In the PREFIX METHOD,
use a left tab for the first number and continue the
left-center-right sequence consecutively.

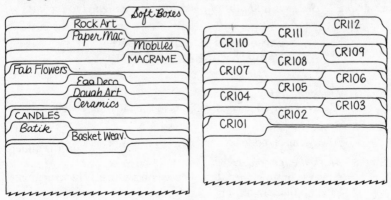

Remember, the maximum number of subjects recommended for the PREFIX METHOD is thirty-five. Therefore, the highest consecutive number possible on the file folders is thirty-five.

Advantages of the PREFIX METHOD

Are there any advantages in using a PREFIX METHOD Paperdex and code? When so few folders are involved, why not simply print the subjects on the folder and file them? There are at least four advantages for using the PREFIX METHOD.

First, the PREFIX METHOD Paperdex provides a central list of subjects filed in the category. Secondly, it provides a place to cite cross reference information within the category, as well as from one category to another. The Paperdex not only is useful in retrieving materials, but in filing them as well.

Third, the prefix letters in the code provide uniformity within a category. Which **CRAFTS FILE** drawer do you think is easier to read?

Fourth, the file folders do not need to be alphabetized when codes are printed on the tabs. The folders always stay neatly in sequence.

The PREFIX METHOD in the File ... Don't Pile system is most effective for smaller categories or mini-files, those with thirty-five or fewer file folders. What happens if a category starts out small, but interest in that area grows and the file expands beyond thirty-five folders? How can one determine initially which method, A-Z METHOD or PREFIX METHOD, is the most appropriate to use for a category? These and other questions are answered in Chapter Seven. Read Chapter Six first on how materials filed in either method can be cross referenced.

Whether it's an oven that needs to be cleaned or a pile of papers that needs to be organized, the longer the task gets postponed, the more reluctant a person becomes to work on it. The old Spanish proverb, "Habits are first cobwebs, then cables," is very true.

Summary
Two Principles of the PREFIX METHOD

Principle 1. *The key to each category is the PREFIX METHOD Paperdex.*

Principle 2. *Subjects and tabs of file folders are assigned to a code.*

Three Steps for Filing Papers
Using the PREFIX METHOD

Step 1. *Mark the index.*
Always enter codes and subjects in the index in pencil.

Step 2. *Mark the item.*
Always mark code on each item so it can be easily refiled.

Step 3. *Mark the file folder.*
Always continue the tab sequence consecutively since the prefix letters remain constant.

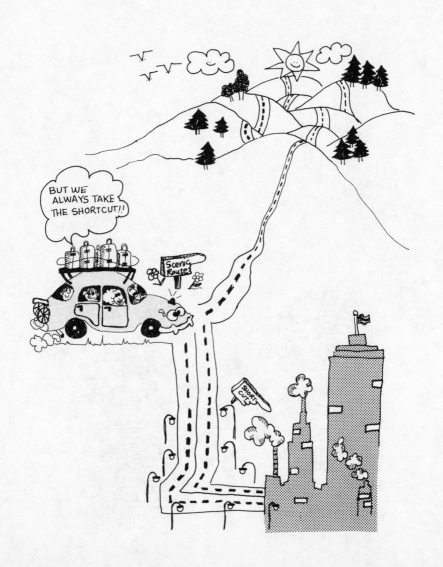

Chapter Six
Take a Right Turn at the Cross Reference

Purposes of Cross Referencing

Have you ever heard it said, "I finally got it all together ... but I forgot where I put it?" What frustration! After putting heart and soul into getting organized, the very *least* the mind can do is cooperate. Unfortunately, our minds don't always think the same way two days in a row. (Sometimes I don't even think the same way twice on the same day.) Once I saw a sign that read, "Everything has been thought of before ... the difficulty is to think of it again." One purpose of cross referencing is **to trigger the mind into remembering.**

A second purpose of cross referencing is **to direct the seeker to information in the file.** It tells a person where to go — in a nice way, of course. A cross reference is like a detour sign. I'm not terribly excited about detours, but if the side trips get me where I need to go, I appreciate having arrows spell out alternative directions. They spare me the hassle of getting lost and save a lot of time. A cross reference, like an arrow on a road sign, can save hours of gnashing teeth.

This chapter discusses three kinds of cross references:

1. **SEE** cross references

2. **SEE ALSO** cross references

3. **REMINDER** cross references

All three types of cross references fulfill these purposes: 1) **to trigger the mind into remembering** and 2) **to direct the seeker to information in the file.** A bonus reason for cross referencing is that it eliminates filing duplicate papers under various subject headings.

SEE Cross References

There are at least three instances when a **SEE** cross reference can be used:

1. **When a subject heading can be referred to by more than one term.**
   Examples:
   Anxiety or *Worry*
   Auto Repair or *Car Repair*
   Pets or *Animals*

2. **When a subject can be interfiled within a broader subject heading.**
   Examples:
   Paris interfiled in *France*
   Mittens interfiled in *Handwear*
   Quiches interfiled in *Egg Dishes*

3. **When an obscure subject or item can be interfiled and there is potential it might be forgotten.** Examples:
   Box Elder Bug Treatment arbitrarily interfiled in *Gardening*
   Newspaper article entitled "Just for Today" arbitrarily interfiled in *Resolutions*

> Instance 1 *When a subject heading can be referred to by more than one term.*

The question is often asked, "How do you choose which subject heading to use, for example, *Appetizers* or *Hors d'oeuvre?"* The answer: *Select the term YOU would most likely look under when wanting specific information.* The File...Don't Pile system doesn't lock you into using predetermined subject headings. The lists of subject headings in the Appendix are only suggestions.

If you commonly refer to a casserole as a hot dish, for example, then *Hot Dishes* is the subject heading under which to file those recipes. If you would think to look under *Curtains* for curtain ideas, select *Curtains* as the subject heading, not *Window Treatment*. What is *Transgression* to one person, may be *Sin* to another. Select the term *you* feel most comfortable using.

Once a subject heading is determined, cite it in the SUBJECT column and assign it a code number in the Paperdex. As you do this, always think about using the file in the future. Will you remember the subject heading you selected tomorrow or next month? If others are using the file, will they think to look under other subject headings for the information you filed? It is wise to cite alternative terms as **SEE** cross references in the Paperdex. The **SEE** cross references will trigger your memory and will thoughtfully direct others where to go to find information you have filed.

A **SEE** cross reference is listed in the right-hand column of the Paperdex for both the A-Z METHOD and the PREFIX METHOD. **ALWAYS WORK IN PENCIL.** The **SEE** column has absolutely no connection with the other columns of the Paperdex. The **SEE** column is reserved strictly as a space to inform the seeker, "Hey, do you want information on such and such a subject? Well, you can have it, but you must look under (or **SEE**) this subject. ... "   Here is an example. A young member of the family wants to make frosting for a cake. In the **COOKING FILE INDEX,** she turns to the "F" page to locate *Frostings.* As she scans the left-hand column, the SUBJECT column, she is unable to find the subject listed. However, in the right-hand column, the **SEE** column, a simple notation instructs her to **SEE** file folder I101 for *Frostings.*

Only the alternate term, *Frostings,* and the code of the subject being referred to, I101, need to be indicated. The seeker needs only to know which file folder to retrieve for the information. Adding the subject, *Icings,* after the code, I101, takes up space in the **SEE** column. It isn't necessary. If one is so curious as to why frosting recipes are filed in I101, he can always look on the "I" page of the Paperdex and learn that I101 *Icings*. Most likely he will go directly to file folder I101.

Start the list of **SEE** cross references at the top of the **SEE** column. Add to the list as needed. Don't worry about alphabetical order. It is easy to scan the column for subject headings.

When cross referencing from one category to another, be sure to indicate in which category the user should refer. Unless otherwise indicated, it is assumed that the **SEE** cross reference falls within the same category.

Instance 2 *When a subject can be interfiled within a broader subject heading.*

It would not be economical or practical to file only one or two items on a subject in one folder, unless the subject has potential for growth. When there are only a few items on a subject, interfile them within a related subject that is broader in scope. For example, if you only have one or two maps or brochures on Arizona, New Mexico, and Utah, file them together under the subject heading *Southwestern States*. Cite the individual states in the **SEE** cross reference column on the appropriate pages of the A-Z METHOD Paperdex.

The File... Don't Pile™ Paperdex™

N

SUBJECT	SEE ALSO	SEE
N101 -Nassau	B104	New Mexico-S105
N102-Norway	O102	New Orleans-L102
N103-Netherlands		
N104-New England		

Similarly in a **COOKING FILE,** if you have many recipes for a specific vegetable, such as potatoes, they would be filed as a separate subject, specifically, P105 *Potatoes*. But if you have only one broccoli recipe, and one spinach recipe, and a few miscellaneous vegetable recipes, it's better to file them together under V101 *Vegetables* and cite the individual vegetables as **SEE** cross references.

The File... Don't Pile™ Paperdex™

B

SUBJECT	SEE ALSO	SEE
B101 -Breads		Broccoli-V101
B102 -Beverage		Bratwurst-S102
B103-Bars/Brownies		
B104-Breakfast		
B105-Beans		

Instance 3 *When an obscure subject or item can be interfiled and there is potential that it might be forgotten.*

In most cases, retrieving materials is fast and easy. It doesn't matter if it has been six weeks or six months since the puppet patterns were filed, for instance. When the patterns are wanted, the subject *Puppets* immediately comes to mind. After simply checking the code in the Paperdex, the corresponding file folder with the patterns can be located.

Most people agree that locating information filed under basic subject headings such as *Prayer, Faith, Tithing,* and *Temptation* is quick and uncomplicated. But the subjects for some items are not so obvious. Retrieval is slower because it is difficult to recall under which subject the item has been filed. A favorite Dear Abby column, "Just for Today," might be filed under R106 *Resolutions.* A month later when it is wanted, all that may come to mind, however, is "Just for Today," not *Resolutions* because that word wasn't in the title. Even searching under the seemingly logical subjects may produce no results. It's frustrating because the article is in the file — it's just "lost" in the file.

The **SEE** cross reference solves the dilemma of "losing" filed information. In this case, a simple notation in the **SEE** column on the "J" page of the Paperdex — such as "Just for Today"-R106 — is all that is needed to immediately trigger one's memory on the location of the article.

I once lived in a house in which I had many great battles with box elder bugs. When I finally learned how to get rid of those pests, I scribbled the solution on a small scrap of paper. Like many people, I promptly taped the note inside my cupboard door, along with 500 other VIPs (Very Important Papers). One day I couldn't stand the mess any longer and decided there had to be a way this valuable information could be filed and not get "lost" in my files.

I selected the most obvious category I had, the **HOMEMAKING FILE,** in which to file the box elder bug memo. Since I didn't have the subjects *Insects* or *Bugs* in this category (and probably never would have), I chose the most logical subject heading, *Gardening,* within which to interfile the scrap of paper. Then I made a notation on the "B" page in the **SEE** column as a cross reference to me to look in G101 the next time I needed that information. The **SEE** cross reference indicates exactly in which folder I have filed the little scrap of paper. Actually, under which subject I chose to interfile the information is irrelevant. The bug solution could be filed under *Puppets* if I chose to do so, and it would still be easy to retrieve. If the **SEE** cross reference tells me to **SEE** P107 for Box Elder Bug Solution, why should I doubt it? Just retrieve the folder, and locate the information.

The File...Don't Pile" Paperdex ™   B

SUBJECT	SEE ALSO	SEE
B101 -Birthday Parties		Bottle Lamps-L105
B102 -Bulletin Boards		Bags- P103
B103 -Basketweaving		Box Elder Bug
B104 -Bookshelves		Solution- G101
		Bookstands-B104

SEE ALSO Cross References

The **SEE ALSO** cross reference is used in one instance:
When additional information about a specific subject can be found under other related subjects.
The **SEE ALSO** column is reserved strictly as a space to inform the seeker, "Hey, look! There's even *more* information about this subject. **SEE ALSO** these related topics." For instance, in a **HOMEMAKING FILE,** materials filed under *Interior Decorating* may provide information you need to redo a room. However, materials filed in other folders on related subjects might also be helpful, for example, *Wallpapering, Painting, Drapes and Curtains, Carpeting and Rugs,* and *Lamps.* If you ignore related topics, you may be missing some valuable ideas that would enhance your decor.

Related subjects are cited as **SEE ALSO** cross references in the Paperdex. Like the **SEE** cross reference, the **SEE ALSO** cross reference triggers the memory, plus it thoughtfully informs others using the file that additional materials concerning the topic are available.

A **SEE ALSO** cross reference is listed in the center column of the Paperdex for both the A-Z METHOD and the PREFIX METHOD. **ALWAYS WORK IN PENCIL.** The **SEE ALSO** column is directly related to the SUBJECT column, because the **SEE ALSO** cross references are cited directly adjacent to the subject to which they are related.

In the **COOKING FILE** below, for example, someone who needed ideas for meals on hot summer days can refer to the main folder, S106 *Summer Cookery* for recipes, but can **SEE ALSO:** B104 *Barbeques;* L102 *Lunch Ideas;* S102 *Sandwiches;* F103 *Frozen Desserts.*

The File . . . Don't Pile™ Paperdex™		S
SUBJECT	SEE ALSO	SEE
S101 - Soups/Stews		
S102 - Sandwiches	L102	
S103 - Salads		
S104 - Scandinavian Cook		
S105 - Sprouting		
S106 - Summer Cookery	B104; L102; S102; F103	

When citing the **SEE ALSO** cross references in the center column, it isn't necessary to include the name of the related subject, only the code number. Including the subject is superfluous and takes up space. The code is sufficient to direct the seeker to the location of the additional related subjects.

When cross referencing from one category to another, be sure to indicate in which category the seeker should refer. Unless otherwise noted, it is assumed that the **SEE ALSO** cross reference is within the same category.

One filer thought it would be a practical idea to color-code the cross references from other categories in the Paperdex. For instance, instead of printing the abbreviation Ckg. below M102, he printed M102 in red which was the color used for the **COOKING FILE.** Unfortunately, when changes became necessary, he was unable to make any alterations in his Paperdex. **ALWAYS WORK IN PENCIL.**

The File . . . Don't Pile™ Paperdex™		E
SUBJECT	SEE ALSO	SEE
E101 - Easter Ideas		Etiquette - M107
E102 - Embroidery		
E103 - Entertaining	M102; N106; P103; Ckg.	

REMINDER Cross References

Another form of cross reference is the **REMINDER** cross reference. There are at least three instances when a **REMINDER** cross reference can be used:

1. **When an item needed is located on the back of or within an article filed under another subject.**

2. **When an item needed is located in a book, either personal or public library.**

3. **When an item needed is too big to fit into a file folder.**

> Instance 1 *When an item needed is located on the back of or within an article filed under another subject.*

To illustrate a typical example of this situation, picture Clever Elsie knitting a sweater. She decides to take a break and picks up the knitting directions which consist of several pages clipped from a *Family Circle* magazine. As she nonchalantly leafs through the instructions, she spies a picture of a fantastic bookshelf on the back of one of the pages. It's love at first sight. She is determined that when the time and money are right, *that* is *the* bookshelf for her. Several days later, when the sweater is finished, the directions are refiled in K102 where they belong. Question: Two years from now when the time and money are finally right, will Clever Elsie remember where she saw the picture of that fantastic bookshelf? Don't bet on it.

Clever Elsie will remember, however, if she takes thirty seconds to make a quick **REMINDER** cross reference note and drops it in file folder, B112 *Bookshelves.*

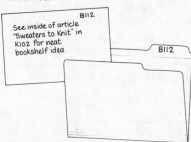

Two years later on Bookshelf Building Day, Elsie simply whips out folder B112 and spies the little **REMINDER** note amongst the myriad bookshelf ideas she's been saving. She retrieves folder K102. As she thumbs through "Sweaters to Knit," she exclaims, "Aha! I remember that fantastic bookshelf idea! It all comes back to me now." Pause. "I don't like it anymore, but there it is!"

Papers can be located an eon after they are filed, if **REMINDER** cross references are dropped in the file folders. The **REMINDER** cross references save time, money, and space. There is no need to duplicate information already filed.

Don't be concerned about losing little pieces of paper from your files. I moved nine times in nine years and never lost any from mine. An alternative, however, if you don't want a lot of 3" x 5" **REMINDER** cross reference cards in a folder, is to tape a sheet of paper inside the file folder and cite these cross references on it.

REMINDER cross references should not be cited directly in the Paperdex because the notes take up too much space. See below:

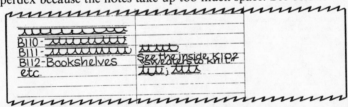

People with photographic memories and instant recall may not need **REMINDER** cross references, but others using the file will have to depend on them to locate the information. A family in Hayward, California, unknowingly helped me realize the value of a good personal filing system. The husband showed me the four-drawer **RELIGION FILE** his wife had set up. When I asked about the system, he told me about his experience in preparing a talk on charity he was to give at his church. He had been surprised that in spite of their extensive file, there wasn't one item on charity. Questioning his wife, she assured him the subject *Charity* was there, he just wasn't looking in the right place. The information was neatly filed under the subject of *Sin*. When he asked her what *Charity* had to do with *Sin,* she responded, "Nothing. It's simply that the first thing I filed years ago on *Charity* happened to be on the back of an article on *Sin,* so I've just kept them all together. It's easy — once you get the hang of it."

> **Instance 2** *When an item needed is located in a book, either personal or public library.*

There are probably favorite passages, poems, recipes, or ideas in your personal books relating to information in your files. You certainly don't want to rip the books apart in order to interfile the information with similar materials. Yet, it would be useful to correlate the information in the books with similar materials in the file. There are often items of interest in public library books that would be resourceful to have on file. It isn't always feasible, however, to duplicate pages from the books. Sometimes the entire book is pertinent, but it might be impossible to have your own copy. In either case, personal or public library books, the **REMINDER** cross reference can help the seeker track down information relating to subjects on file.

Mary Brown has been asked to bring a salad to a salad smorgasbord. In order to decide which salad to take, she retrieves folders S110 and S111 from her **COOKING FILE.** One folder is for fruit salads, and one is for vegetable salads. The two folders provide Mary access to all of the salad recipes in her cookbooks as well. The **REMINDER** cross references inform her of the names of the recipes, in which cookbooks they can be found, and the page numbers.

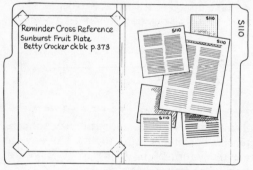

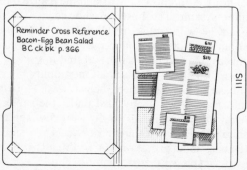

Sally Smith finds an excellent library book on children's birthday parties. She makes a **REMINDER** cross reference note and drops it in file folder B105 for *Birthday Party Ideas.*

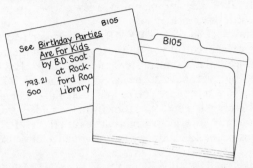

Instance 3 *When an item needed is too big to fit into a file folder.*

Materials in my files are not limited to thin sheets of paper. I file thin paperbacks and pamphlets as well as thick maps and brochures. If the item, such as an envelope with patterns in it, is too bulky to fit into a file folder, yet can be put into a file drawer, I file it directly behind the folder and indicate the code on the envelope. Some materials, however, are simply too big to fit into a file folder. A **REMINDER** cross reference helps one to find large items stored in other locations.

When the October leaves start to crunch, it's a sure sign my children will dig into the files for *Halloween.* Pictures, party and game ideas, recipes, costume patterns, stories, and many ideas saved year after year are easy to tuck into file folders. But what about the beanbag pumpkins, jack-o-lantern candles, and big plastic trick-or-treat buckets? Jot a note on a **REMINDER** cross reference card and drop it into the file folder of Halloween ideas.

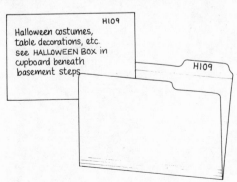

This is part of what putting a house in order is all about. No, I have not arrived, but it is exciting to be working on it. It brings a sense of satisfaction and security knowing where to find what you want when you need it. It takes time and planning (a few shelves are handy, too), but it's well worth the effort.

The only drawback in filing a **REMINDER** cross reference, such as the above example, occurs if you move. If your new home doesn't have a cupboard beneath the basement steps and you put the Halloween box in the garage attic, you have to be sure to change the **REMINDER** cross reference. If you are sure you're well rooted and will never move, **REMINDER** cross references filed directly in the folders work great. If you move frequently, an effective alternative is to file the **REMINDER** cross references in the Location section of your Rolodex (see Chapter Eight).

Whether it is a **SEE,** a **SEE ALSO,** or a **REMINDER** cross reference, the rule of thumb on when to cite these notes is: **Write down the cross references when you think of them.** This can occur either when you are filing or when you are retrieving materials. Remember the old Chinese proverb, "Even faded ink is better than the worst memory." Write it down! You won't forget, and others using the files will appreciate it, too.

Summary
Purposes for Cross Referencing

1. To trigger the mind into remembering.
2. To direct the seeker to information in the file.

Kinds of Cross References

1. SEE Cross References (cited in far right-hand column of Paperdex). They are used:

    a. When a subject heading can be referred to by more than one term.

    b. When a subject can be interfiled within a broader subject heading.

    c. When an obscure subject or item can be interfiled and there is potential that it might be forgotten.

2. SEE ALSO Cross References (cited in center column of Paperdex). They are used: When additional information about a specific subject can be found under related subjects.

3. REMINDER Cross References (cited on cards filed directly into folders). They are used:

    a. When an item needed is located on the back of or within an article filed under another subject.

    b. When an item needed is located in a book, either personal or public library.

    c. When an item needed is too big to fit into a file folder.

Chapter Seven
Divide and Conquer

Plan of Attack

Think of it! After years and years of accumulating, stashing and piling, this is the end of fumbling from one filing system to another. Look no more. Grab your shovel, Utopia is in sight!

But wait! You've been accumulating treasures for twenty-five years. Which category are you going to work on first? You don't plan to tackle all of your papers at once, do you? That would be like spring cleaning your entire house — walls, drapes, carpets, closets — in every room on one day. Even Breathless Broom Service would have to recruit extra help to accomplish that feat. A more sane arrangement would be to have a plan of attack.

For a more systematic approach, first duplicate the Plan of Attack Chart on the next page. Complete the chart as directed.

Complete Columns One, Two, and Three first for all categories listed.

1. Column One - BROAD CATEGORIES
   List categories to be filed as they appear on the preliminary Priorities List described in Chapter Three.
   After the categories are listed in Column One, the preliminary list can be thrown away.

2. Column Two - PAPERS CENTRALIZED
   Check off each category when papers are centralized, for example, if travel papers are strewed in ten locations, don't check Column Two until they are centralized together.

3. Column Three - METHOD/COLOR
   Indicate which method and color will be used for each category, for example, A-Z/red or PREFIX/blue. This chapter will help clarify

how to determine which method is best to use for a particular category.

When Columns One, Two, and Three are completed, check off Columns Four and Five as each category is organized. FILE *ONE* CATEGORY AT A TIME.

4. Column Four - PAPERDEX SET UP

5. Column Five - SYSTEM STARTED

Check off each category when a Paperdex and a file have been established. To determine how many Paperdexes are needed, total the methods listed in Column Three, for example, four A-Z METHOD, ten PREFIX METHOD.

To obtain preprinted Paperdexes, use the order form at the back of this book.

	BROAD CATEGORIES	PAPERS CENTRALIZED	METHOD/ COLOR	PAPERDEX SET UP	SYSTEM STARTED
1.					
2.					
3.					
4.					
5.					
6.					
7.					
8.					
9.					
10.					

PLAN OF ATTACK CHART

The Plan of Attack Chart is like a road map. It provides a sense of direction to organize papers. The chart not only indicates what is planned to be done, but how it will be accomplished and serves as a progress record. Tape the chart inside this book or frame it and hang it above the desk. Don't lose it. By the time the last category on the list is filed, the chart will be a symbol of great sweat and sacrifice. Who knows, maybe it should be bronzed! A complete Plan of Attack Chart based on the examples given in Chapter Three looks like this:

PLAN OF ATTACK CHART

	BROAD CATEGORIES	PAPERS CENTRALIZED	METHOD/ COLOR	PAPERDEX SET UP	SYSTEM STARTED
1.	Homemaking	✓	A-Z/Red	✓	✓
2.	Cooking	✓	A-Z/Blue	✓	✓
3.	Personal Interest (Barb)	✓	Prefix/Green	✓	✓
4.	Personal Interest (Bob)	✓	Prefix/Brown	✓	✓
5.	Jill/Bill	✓	Prefix/Orange Prefix/Black	✓	✓
6.	Nursing	✓	Prefix/Purple	✓	✓
7.	Religion	✓	A-Z/Green	✓	✓
8.	Genealogy	✓	Prefix/Blue	✓	✓
9.	Travel	✓	A-Z/Brown	✓	✓
10.	Personal Business	✓	Prefix/Black	✓	✓

A-Z METHOD or PREFIX METHOD?

How do you determine which method, A-Z or PREFIX, is the best to use for a particular category? Selecting the filing method generally depends on two factors.

> Factor 1 *The amount of material accumulated or might be accumulated in a given category.*

Let's use papers concerning the topic of camping to illustrate how to decide the filing method.

The A-Z METHOD Option

If you have boxes and boxes of papers concerning camping, the method to use is the A-Z METHOD. Papers can be filed quickly in a **CAMPING FILE** by determining the subject of each item, citing the subject on the appropriate page in the Paperdex and printing the corresponding code on a file folder. The "F" page might include such subjects as: *First Aid, Fishing, Fire Building, Farm Pond Camping,* and *Fuel Safety.*

If you only have a small number of papers about camping, but realize your interest in it is increasing, you probably will accumulate more papers concerning it in the future. It is best to use the A-Z METHOD because *the category has potential for growth.*

The PREFIX METHOD Option

On the other hand, if you have a small box of papers concerning the topic of camping and don't anticipate accumulating much more, the method to use is the PREFIX METHOD.

The usual way people handle this amount of material is to overload one or two file folders and label them *Camping Stuff.* Whenever information is needed for an outing, they plow through the bulging mess trying to find what they want.

Instead, treat the topic of camping as a mini-category, one that can include as few as five file folders or as many as thirty-five.

The File . . . Don't Pile™ Paperdex™		CMP Camping
SUBJECT	**SEE ALSO**	**SEE**
CMP101 -Camp. Equipm't		Tents-CMP101
CMP102-Backpacking		Fire Building-
CMP103-Camp. Facilities		CMP105
CMP104- Bicycling		Hostels-CMP103
CMP105- Safety		Campgrounds-
CMP106- First Aid		CMP103
etc.		Fuel Safety-CMP105

The Final Option
(next to throwing the stuff away)

Maybe you are a casual or beginning camper and only have enough papers concerning camping to fill one file folder. It doesn't warrant using the PREFIX METHOD and certainly not the A-Z METHOD. Yet, there is the little pile of papers. Where do you put *one* file folder?

In this case, treat the papers as a subject, *Camping,* not a broad category, CAMPING. File the subject, *Camping,* within the most logical category you have, i.e., TRAVEL; RECREATION; PERSONAL INTEREST; SPORTS. When I first started filing, I filed *Camping* in HOMEMAKING because it was my most logical category established.

> Factor 2 *The uniqueness of the material accumulated.*

Sometimes it isn't a matter of quantity that determines which method to use. For instance, as a school librarian, I had boxes and boxes of professional papers on the topic of LIBRARY. If I had only adhered to Factor 1, it would have seemed logical to file such a quantity in the A-Z METHOD. However, in analyzing the materials, the papers fell into three distinct categories — 1) LIBRARY ADMINISTRATION, 2) LIBRARY SKILLS, and 3) STORIES. This breakdown didn't decrease the amount of paper, but it shifted it into three more manageable piles to be filed. Let's further analyze one of these categories, LIBRARY ADMINISTRATION, to illustrate how the uniqueness of materials can affect the choice of filing method.

The box of papers included major subdivisions such as General Administration, Reading Guidance, Library Programs, Publicity, Print Materials, and Nonprint Materials and Equipment. Each subdivision involved several subjects. If the A-Z METHOD had been used, the subjects from each subdivision would have been interfiled with each other, for example, *Budgeting, Book Week,* and *Bibliographies* would have been on the "B" page. I wanted to treat each subdivision separately, yet maintain all of them under the major category, LIBRARY ADMINISTRATION.

An adaptation of the PREFIX METHOD permitted this because all of the papers used the same prefix letters, L/AD, for LIBRARY ADMINISTRATION. However, because each subdivision was assigned a block of code numbers, the subjects within each subdivision could be filed together as a group. For example, here are six subdivisions in the category LIBRARY ADMINISTRATION, the block of numbers assigned and a sample of the subjects.

L/AD100-199 - **General Administration**
L/AD100 - *Annual Reports*
L/AD101 - *Budgeting*
L/AD102 - *Library Standards*
L/AD103 - *Selecting Policies*
L/AD104 - *Ordering Mechanics*
L/AD105 - *Censorship Policy*
L/AD106 - *Withdrawal Policy*
L/AD107 - *Library Council*
L/AD200-299 - **Reading Guidance,** including such subjects as *Caldecott Books, Newbery Books, Bibliographies, Beginning Readers, Bibliotherapy, Illustrators,* and *Children's Literature.*
L/AD300-399 - **Library Programs,** including materials concerning *Book Week, Library Week, Book Fairs and Festivals, Read-a-thons,* and *Junior Great Books Reading Program.*
L/AD400-499 - **Publicity,** including promotional methods such as *Bulletin Board Ideas, Exhibits and Displays, Newsletter Ideas,* and *News Releases.*
L/AD500-599 - **Print Materials,** including *Book Selection Sources, Magazine Selection Sources, Vertical File Selection Sources, Cataloging and Processing,* and *Book Mending and Binding.*
L/AD600-699 - **Nonprint Materials and Equipment,** including *Film Selection Sources, Filmstrip Selection Sources, Records and Tapes Selection Sources, Cataloging and Processing, In-Service Training, Nonprint Materials Production,* and *Equipment Selection and Maintenance.*

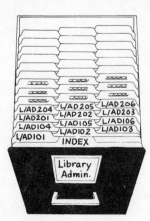

The large block of numbers assigned to each subdivision allowed ample room for growth and permitted a distinct division. When an unhappy parent was on the phone, it was as easy to locate the censorship policy as it was to find materials when making plans for Book Week.

Papers for other professions and personal interests can use a similar adaptation of the PREFIX METHOD. In one of my classes a freelance writer brainstormed with me about her various ongoing projects. We discovered that each of her projects followed the same sequence: *Budding Idea, Research, Drafts, Final Copy, Correspondence,* and *Published Copies.* Here is how three of her current projects were treated as mini-categories. Each writing project was assigned prefix letters, for example, **PUPPETRY-PUP; WALKING-WLK; BARTERING-BAR.** Since each category only involved six folders, all three categories were entered on one Paperdex sheet.

The File... Don't Pile" Paperdex™   PUP;WLK;BAR

SUBJECT	SEE ALSO	SEE
PUP101 - Budding Idea		
PUP102 - Research		
PUP103 - Drafts		
PUP104 - Final Copy		
PUP105 - Correspondence		
PUP106 - Published Copies		
WLK101 - Budding Idea		
WLK102 - Research		
WLK103 - Drafts		
WLK104 - Final Copy		
WLK105 - Correspondence		
WLK106 - Published Copies		
BAR101 - Budding Idea		
BAR102 - Research		
BAR103 - Drafts		
BAR104 - Final Copy		
BAR105 - Correspondence		
BAR106 - Published Copies		

Each draft of the project can be filed separately if desired by adding a small subscript letter to the code, for example, $PUP103_a$, $PUP103_b$, $PUP103_c$. However, the same tab position should be maintained so the tabs of the folders stay in sequence.

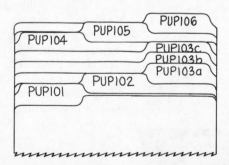

Determine which method is the most suitable for the papers you are saving. But be aware that as time passes and interests change and grow, so can the papers in your files. A subject filed in one folder under the A-Z METHOD can blossom into its own mini-category. Initially it was for personal reasons that I saved information on the subject of time management. The amount of papers I had fit into one folder in my **HOMEMAKING FILE.** When I became professionally involved in time management seminars, the amount of material I accumulated increased. The papers are now filed according to the PREFIX METHOD with TM as the prefix letters for the category **TIME MANAGEMENT.** Subject breakdown includes, for example, *Goal Setting, Priorities, Scheduling,* and *Time Robbers.*

The Master Index

A student in a File ... Don't Pile workshop teased me one night and asked if I had an index to my indexes. I responded, "A Master Index?! That's bordering on fanatic!" When the same challenge was repeated in more workshops, I began to reflect on how my files had developed, and I realized the importance of the question.

Years ago when I started the File ... Don't Pile System, I didn't have a Plan of Attack Chart. My categories developed one or two at a time. At first, I only had two categories, **RELIGION** and **HOMEMAKING.** I learned from my mistake of incorporating the topic of cooking as part of my **HOMEMAKING FILE.** The subjects on the "B" page of my Paperdex jumped from *Batik* to *Breads* to *Basketweaving* to *Beverages.* It was a confusing conglomeration. It wasn't long before the **COOKING FILE** became a separate category. The **PERSONAL BUSINESS FILE** was created one tax season as I was centralizing receipts and other important papers.

Because my list of categories evolved over a period of time, I became familiar with my files as they were added. Your perspective, however, like the perspectives of filing workshop students, is unique to you. The preliminary steps outlined in Chapter Three focus you immediately on the *total* picture of what categories you need to file. More categories will develop later. When your files are set up, the Plan of Attack Chart can be thrown away. Consequently, the only list of your categories is in your head.

My answer now when asked about an index to my indexes is "Yes, the Master Index." *The Master Index is one step beyond the Plan of Attack Chart and, in a limited way, is like a small computer.* It indicates the names of the categories, how each is filed (Method/Color), general contents of each category and location of the file. It can be kept at a central place such as on the desk. The format of the Master Index can be on 8½" x 11" chart or on Rolodex cards (see Chapter Eight). If you own a home computer, program the Master Index on it.

MASTER INDEX			
FILE (BROAD CATEGORY)	METHOD/ COLOR	GENERAL CONTENTS	LOCATION
1. Homemaking	A-Z/Red	gardening; needlepoint; crafts; child development; sewing; decorating	3rd drawer, 4 dwr. cab.
2. Cooking	A-Z/Blue	recipes; diets; nutrition; menu planning	Kitchen
3. Personal Interest (Barb)	Prefix (PI)/Green	Women's Club; Hosp. Aux.; PTA; Book Club; Quilters Assn; calligraphy; tennis; exercise/beauty tips	File drawer Barb's desk
4. Personal Interest (Bob)	Prefix (PI)/Brown	Lion's Club; Am. Dental Assn; photography; golf; sailing	File drawer Bob's desk
5. Jill File Bill File	Prefix (JL)/Orange Prefix (BL)/Black	School papers; cards; letters	Share 2nd dwr. in 4 dwr. cab.
6. Nursing	Prefix (Nsg)/Purple	Class notes; resume; job hunting info.	File drawer Barb's desk
7. Religion	A-Z/Green	Poems; quotes; inspirational articles	Top drawer 4 dwr. cab.
8. Genealogy	Prefix (Gen)/Blue	Reference material; maps; class notes; (research kept in binders)	Bottom dwr. 4 dwr. cab.
9. Travel	A-Z/Brown	Maps; brochures; camping info.	Bottom dwr. 4 dwr. cab.
10. Personal Business	Prefix (PB)/Black	Tax papers; insurance; birth certs; health recs; Fluffy's rec; sales receipts war./quar.	File drawer Bob's desk

A Master Index is useful in assisting others using the files. It designates under which category subjects are filed and where the files are located. At a glance the Master Index shows how many files you have established *and helps prevent your files from increasing to the point where you have more files than furniture.* This leads to the issues of how long information should be retained in the files and how often the files should be weeded.

Throw ... Don't Stow!

A woman who informed her family that she had signed up for the File ... Don't Pile workshop was told, "Mother, you don't need that class. You need to take 'Throw ... Don't Stow!'" Many people who take the filing workshop or who buy this book suffer from "Crammed-Attic Cramps" which develop from a common cause — the willingness to keep every piece of paper created. The cramps become more intense over a longer period of time, if not treated properly.

In his book, *Fat Paper*, Lee Grossman correlates the problem of fat files with those of fat people. If people don't control their intake when they eat, they become fat. Files that ingest a lot of paper on an uncontrolled basis also become fat. Losing weight requires a thoughtful diet, nerve, and, for lasting results, an awareness of being fat. To keep paperwork reduced, it requires a thoughtful diet, nerve, and an awareness of how the files got fat in the first place. Chapter Two deals with the psychological reasons people pile papers. This chapter explains how to decide what papers should be retained, and for what period of time, plus how to periodically weed files to keep them trim.

It isn't hard to picture why unrestricted paper growth can quickly lead to a storage problem, not to mention a fire hazard. When the basement and attic get full, junk spills into the garage. A student in a filing workshop shared her experience of helping her parents move from their home of twenty-five years. The family spent two months transferring belongings to the new house. The closing date neared and still there was a lot to remove. Before they finished, she said, they loaded five garbage dumpsters with boxes of papers that had been stacked in the house, garage, and two outbuildings. Did the situation change the parents in their new home? No, the recreation room is piled high with papers and can't be used. The two-car garage is so full the cars must be parked outside. According to Don Aslett in *Is There Life After Housework?* there is a Law of the Packrat. It is, "Junk will accumulate proportionately to the storage room available for it."

The problem is further complicated by the rising cost of storage. While business offices are continually aware of the expenses involved in maintaining files, homeowners, on the other hand, don't usually break down the cost of storing their "treasures" per square foot.

In March, 1979, *Changing Times* published a report prepared by Runzheimer and Company, a management consulting firm that compiles cost-of-living data. The study determined housing costs for two families in two different locations in the United States. The first family included four members earning $38,000 gross and living in a seven-room, four-bedroom, two-and-one-half bath house of 2,250 square feet. The second family included two members earning $18,000 gross and living in a five-room, three-bedroom, one-bath house of 1,100 square feet. Principal and interest payment on the home mortgage, insurance, utilities, regular maintenance, and real property taxes as assessed locally were figured in the housing costs. The results indicated that, due to the variation in cost of living in their area of the country, in both cases it cost the families approximately $3 to $9 per square foot to live in their homes. [I assume these are yearly figures, although this wasn't stated.]

If you are using a spare bedroom to stash piles of paper and boxes of magazines, you are paying a fairly expensive storage fee for the space.

Retention Schedule

Once papers are organized in files, a systematic method is needed to control the amount of paper stored. The answer is not sporadic pitching sprees. Business offices use a system called a Records Retention Schedule. While such schedules are generally based on legal requirements, a similar plan can be adapted for home use. Whether for business or home use, the schedule involves deciding how long papers should be kept and where they should be stored.

To develop a retention schedule for home use, follow three steps. (This discussion does not include papers such as cancelled checks, taxes, documents, or sale receipts. These kinds of paper will be covered in Chapter Nine concerning the **PERSONAL BUSINESS FILE.**)

Step 1. Identify who is responsible for setting up the retention schedule.

In some households, the wife is the saver and the husband throws everything out. In other homes, the opposite is true. In either case, pitching season rarely occurs when both parties are present at the same time.

Many people also qualify as both "savers" and "pitchers." They follow an interesting and typical pattern of cleaning out their collections. My mother is a "saver-pitcher." When I was a child, she would reach a "brink" in her saving cycle. On a bright Saturday morning, often without warning, pitching fever would strike. Unless my sister, my brother, and I remained within range, many of our "treasures" would disappear with her discards. After the fever passed, we lapsed into the saving cycle again. Now that I have little savers of my own and realize I, too, am a "saver-pitcher," I empathize with my mother!

Is it a joint decision in your household which papers are saved and which ones are tossed? Or does one person make the decisions — with repercussions such as, "Why were *my* love letters thrown away?!"

If you have just assumed a position in a volunteer organization, in what condition did you receive your predecessor's file? Does the file contain every paper acquired since the organization was founded? Who decides how long papers should be kept? If no one assumes the responsibility, the file will probably continue to grow and be handed down from leader to leader.

The first step in setting up a schedule is to identify who is responsible for deciding how long papers should be kept. A joint decision may be necessary for papers in some categories. Personal files should be decided by the individual who owns them. However, be aware of young people as overzealous savers. They have a simple response to the length of time they plan to save their papers: Forever. If you are of this nature, it might be wise to ask someone to assist you in setting up a schedule.

Step 2. Determine the value of the papers to be stored.

How do you put a price tag on a bundle of letters from Great-Grandmother Sadie? Who can decide the usefulness of a quotation or recipe or pattern? Placing a value on personal papers is a difficult, if not impossible, task. To a saver, *every* paper is important. Yet, there are degrees of importance. To determine the value of papers to be stored, answer three questions.

1. What papers absolutely cannot be replaced?

There are papers in your life that are irreplaceable. Once destroyed, no amount of money or time can restore them. They might include old letters, children's school papers, journals or diaries, old family *Bibles,* memorabilia, creative ideas such as sketches, a manuscript for a book, research information for a project, or a musical composition. The value of such paperwork is precious, and, in some cases, vital.

As a genealogist, I've learned to appreciate the value of vital records. I've experienced the disappointment when key documents are missing. But, I have also felt the joy when information I've needed is available because a vital record has been preserved.

Determine which papers in your life have great importance. What papers are irreplaceable? Compile a list.

2. What papers can be replaced with time and money?

It would seem discouraging if I had to begin my years of genealogical research all over again, but it would be possible. Fortunately, most of the work has been microfilmed or photocopied, so replacing it would be fairly simple.

Most papers can be replaced if a person is willing to spend the time, energy, and money to get them. I loaned my favorite dollhouse pattern to a friend, and the experience taught me a valuable lesson. My friend was sad to inform me that she had somehow misplaced the pattern. Since it had been my only copy and my daughter's dollhouse was half built, I felt even worse. We eventually found a copy of the magazine from which the pattern came, but not without a great deal of trouble. It didn't ruin our friendship and I am still willing to share, but now whenever I loan special papers, I keep my copy and give others a duplicate.

Since I have thousands of newspaper and magazine clippings, it would be impossible for me to ever restore my files if they were destroyed. I would miss many of the papers and would attempt to replace some of them, but not everything. As fun and useful as the information is, it really isn't as important to me as the papers I've classified as "vital."

Determine which papers in your life are important, but replaceable. Compile a general list, for example, recipes, religion articles, travel maps and brochures, arts and crafts patterns, and so forth.

3. What papers are nonessential and do not need to be replaced?

Unless you are a hardcore refunder, if store coupons are lost, life goes on. Just as nonessential are theater and orchestra brochures, seasonal catalogs, and continuing education class schedules. Ephemeral materials are classified nonessential because they are short lived. I consider my travel maps nonessential because there are probably more up-to-date ones available if I did need to replace them. On the other hand, I classify my genealogy maps as "irreplaceable" items because many are historical and technical and would be difficult to acquire again. It's a matter of personal priority. An avid globetrotter would place a higher premium on a scenic tour map of Berlin, Germany, than a territorial map of the Kingdom of Prussia.

Step 3. Determine how long papers should be kept and where they should be stored.

Some people use high tide to determine how long papers should be retained. When the basement floods, it's time to start pitching. For others, moving day is the key motivator. I can identify with that, especially with back issues of magazines. I've decided to follow Don Aslett's advice in *Is There Life After Housework?* He described the 70-30 Law made famous by a magazine publisher. An average magazine is 70 percent advertising. Aslett says, "The first time you read a magazine, remove any article of interest to you and throw the 70% junk away. . . . Instead of piles of magazines, you will have a thin, usable file of articles you want or need. Other junk can be treated the same way, and you'll see a great transformation."

We retain papers for nostalgic reasons to hand down from one generation to the next. Sometimes sentimental value increases with the length of time a piece of paper is saved. We retain papers for reference purposes and often rationalize the length of time we keep them by saying, "I might need that someday."

To determine how long and where to store papers, consider their value. Papers of vital importance should never be destroyed. How can they be safeguarded? Even sleeping with them under your pillow every night won't insure their safety. But, three measures can be taken.

1. *Duplicate the papers whenever possible.* A photocopy of a diary or old letters will not be as precious as the originals, but at least information in them won't be lost.

2. *Keep the duplicate copy away from your home.* If your home is destroyed, you'll be grateful to have copies of irreplaceable papers.

3. *Keep the original in as safe a place as possible.* Items can be stored in a trunk by the door or in the bottom drawer of a metal filing cabinet.

Safeguarding precious papers doesn't mean they have to be buried. If the papers are hidden for fear they might be lost, they will never be in view to be enjoyed as they should. A preconceived plan may save irreplaceable originals in the event of an emergency evacuation. Make a list of items that should be taken and keep several empty peach crates handy to make removal easy.

Papers classified as "replaceable" can be evaluated in terms of contribution. The following questions may be considered.

1. *How frequently is the paper used?*
Some people put an "x" at the top of the paper each time it is removed from the file. Many of my recipes bear telltale signs that indicate their usage.

2. *Is there a copy of the item available elsewhere?*
If an item isn't used too frequently and you don't have room to store it, get rid of it. You can always go to the library if you need the information.

3. *How timely is the information?*
Always date each item filed and this question will be easy to answer. Determine the number of years you feel information will be current and let this be your guideline of how long to retain them. Even new cooking products and equipment may affect the usefulness of recipes that seemingly never would become outdated.

Papers usually fall in three groups in terms of usage — Active Files, Semi-Active Files, and Inactive or Dead Files. Assuming the top and bottom drawers are the most difficult for people to reach, many offices use them to store less active files. The middle two drawers are reserved for the most frequently used or active files. Adapt this procedure to fit your personal needs. In my case, I use the bottom drawers of two cabinets to store the very active **STORY FILE** and **GAME FILE** because my children can reach those drawers. In another cabinet, I store back issues of a magazine to which I absolutely will not put a scissors. The magazines are heavy so the bottom drawer is the best place to store them even though I refer to them frequently.

Inactive Files should not be stored in expensive steel cabinets. Less costly storage boxes made of heavy cardboard are serviceable. I classify my professional papers from former teaching days and old college notebooks as dead materials. While I don't refer to them frequently, I also don't want to discard them.

Nonessential papers can be filed within different categories. Many can be considered pending (see Chapter Eight) and have expiration dates. They are retained until acted upon or the expiration date passes. Other nonessential papers are filed in the category of their interest, for example, **MONEY MANAGEMENT, PERSONAL INTEREST,** and **TRAVEL.** This leads to the Weeding Process which is the means of periodically cleaning out nonessential papers from files.

Weeding Process

Files, like gardens, need to be weeded and pruned periodically. Items need to be discarded that have either been filed by accident or in a moment of poor judgment, as well as those that have served their purpose and have outlived their span of importance. Some papers may not be relevant to new personal interests or changed opinions. Redundant information is just that!

But weeds and unwanted papers do not self-destruct. You have to work at it! Is there a systematic approach to weeding files? An annual spring check-up can keep your files in a healthy, trim condition. If you have several files, this can be a time-consuming task. Here are some suggestions to make the job easier.

1. **Weed only one file or category at a time.**

2. **Use the Ten Criteria Questions listed in Chapter One.**

3. **Keep a record of when you last weeded the file. This can be noted in the Master Index, if you wish.**

4. **Keep others in mind as you weed out items. If materials aren't outdated and could benefit someone else, share your garbage can with them!**

Summary
Plan of Attack Chart

1. List categories in the order of urgency for filing.
2. Centralize papers in each category.
3. Determine method and color for each category.
4. Establish a Paperdex one category at a time.
5. File papers using the system one category at a time.

Determining Factors of Filing Method

1. The amount of material accumulated or might be accumulated.
2. The uniqueness of the material accumulated.

Master Index

1. List category or files established.
2. Indicate method and color used for each category.
3. Cite general contents of each category.
4. Indicate the location of each file.

Retention Schedule

Step 1. Identify who is responsible for setting up retention schedule.
Step 2. Determine the value of papers to be stored.
Step 3. Determine how long papers should be kept and where they should be stored.

Weeding Process

1. Weed one category at a time.
2. Use Ten Criteria Questions.
3. Keep a Weeding Record.
4. Share weeded items if applicable.

Chapter Eight
Getting Through Each Day

Pending Papers

A versatile piece of equipment in the average home is the refrigerator/freezer. In some households it stores food, laundry, modeling clay, vital papers, and photo film. Without a refrigerator, many homes would be without a bulletin board, which is generally where people post papers to get them through each day.

The single, most frustrating kinds of papers people cope with daily are those that require action, *pending papers*. There are two widely used methods of handling pending papers. One method supports the "out of sight, out of mind" theory. Many people believe that if important notices, bills, anniversary cards, or birthday party invitations are filed in a cabinet, they are sure to be forgotten. Consequently, the wall near the phone and the cupboard doors are plastered full of notes and the counter top is piled high with expired deadlines. Life would be much easier for them if someone would invent a refrigerator door made of solid cork!

The other method is used by people who tuck pending papers in a calendar book so they'll be sure to have them when they need them. The binding of the calendar wheezes and falls apart, and yet more pending items and "to do" lists are added to the bulging mess. Both methods suffer from the common dilemma of papers getting buried and lost in the shuffle. Pending papers, like nonpending papers, can become clutter, too, except there is usually a higher price to pay.

In Chapter Three, the Centralizing Step described the ABC approach to cleaning up paper clutter: A) Get boxes, B) Label boxes, and C) Fill boxes. During the Centralizing Step, one of the boxes, the **PENDING** box, serves as a temporary dropoff point for papers requiring daily action. The box is kept in an accessible location so that pending papers can be easily added or retrieved. It eliminates cluttering the kitchen counter tops with "to do" papers such as an application form, a magazine renewal, and a registration blank for a night class. The **PENDING** box, however, is only a means to an end. Just as nonpending papers centralized in boxes eventually are filed in a systematic order, pending papers also need to be efficiently organized.

The Action Notebook

The method offices use to organize pending papers is called a day file. It is also known as a tickler file, a desk file, or an action file. Whatever the name, its purpose is to serve as a central storage place for papers requiring action.

A commercial desk file sold in office supply stores is like a perpetual calendar in expandable book form. The first section of the book is divided 1-31 for the days of the month and the last section is divided January-December. Each of the 8" x 10" tagboard pages has a celluloid protected tab.

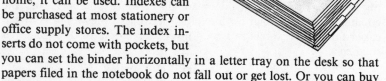

A less expensive means of achieving the same effect is to use a 3-ring binder that has a front and back pocket. Insert two sets of indexes, one tabbed 1-31 and the other, January-December. If you have an extra notebook binder at home, it can be used. Indexes can be purchased at most stationery or office supply stores. The index inserts do not come with pockets, but you can set the binder horizontally in a letter tray on the desk so that papers filed in the notebook do not fall out or get lost. Or you can buy indexed pocket inserts and add acetate tabs.

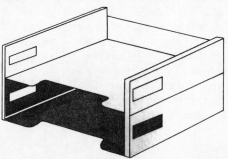

Here are six examples of papers requiring action:

1. Bill for Midwest Power Co. - due April 15
2. Magazine renewal form - due April 30
3. Tickets for concert at Orchestra Hall - April 20
4. Birthday party invitation (including detailed map and directions) for daughter Amy to attend - April 13
5. Card for Mom and Dad's anniversary - April 16
6. Registration receipt needed for Ann's night class - April 13

Here is how the Action Notebook serves as the "home" for these pending papers:

1. File bill for Midwest Power Company behind the 13th. Two days is sufficient travel time for local mail. Allow four or five days for out of state mail.
2. File magazine renewal form behind the 25th.
3. After noting the concert on your calendar, file tickets for concert at Orchestra Hall behind the 20th.
4. After noting the birthday party on your calendar, file the invitation and directions behind the 13th.
5. File the card for Mom and Dad's anniversary behind the 11th.
6. File the registration receipt for Ann's night class behind the 13th.

Each day check your Action Notebook for papers that need to be acted upon that day. I generally do this, as well as check my calendar, the night before so I know what needs to be done the next day. Using the above example, it is clear to see that April 13th involves three actions: 1) the Midwest Power bill is going to be sent. 2) Amy is going to attend a birthday party; there is no worry about finding the house because the directions are ready and waiting. And 3) Ann is going to be able to attend her night class because she has her registration receipt.

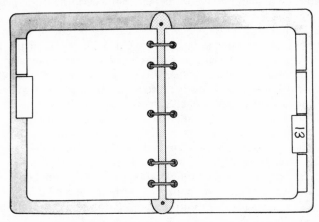

During the month of April, you will probably accumulate pending papers that won't require action until May or even later months. For instance, the deadline for an application blank to set up a booth for a Spring Bazaar might be May 10. Instructions concerning Kindergarten Roundup might not be needed until May 15. File these papers behind the May index tab in the January-December section of the Action Notebook. On the last day of April, remove all of the pending papers for the month of May, determine the dates of action and file them behind the appropriate dates in the 1-31 section of the Action Notebook.

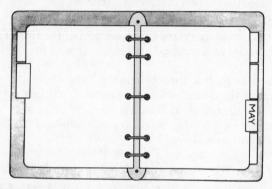

Alan Lakein's time management book, *How to Get Control of Your Time and Your Life* presents the ABC Priority System to evaluate activities and goals. Lakein suggests that "A" activities have a high value, "B" have a medium value, and "C" have a low value. Pending papers in the Action Notebook can be similarly evaluated. Some papers require immediate attention. They are "must do" papers. Other papers are less urgent. They are "should do" papers. Still others are mere considerations and are "could do" papers. For example, an "A" pending paper might be to deposit a check you just received, a "B" item, a bill due the 10th, and a "C" paper, a survey card to be completed for the Department of Transportation. Put "A" pending items in the front pocket of the binder. Whenever the Action Notebook is opened, "A" papers are immediately accessible. "C" items can be kept in the back pocket of the binder. "B" items are filed in the index sections behind the date or month they should be acted upon.

Some people use the Action Notebook as the hub for family activities. While a calendar is essential, a **Schedule Section** can be added in the Action Notebook in which to include school calendars, basketball practices, game schedules and dance lessons.

I have a section in my Action Notebook called the **Sunday Section.** During the week as I acquire papers concerning church business that I need to act on, I put them in this section. If I need to see someone at church, someone to whom I must give or someone from whom I must receive information, I make a note of it in the **Sunday Section**. On Saturday night, I check the **Sunday Section** to collect all of the "to do" papers and notes for the next day.

A **Spouse Section** can serve as a place to put papers your husband or wife should see first before the items are filed. This section is especially effective if your spouse travels out of town and can only read the mail once a week.

If you own a business in your home, have a separate Action Notebook for it. By keeping professional pending papers separate from personal pending papers, you'll be more efficient and successful in accomplishing your goals.

People who live by the "out of sight, out of mind" theory may feel concerned that if they file papers in the Action Notebook, they'll forget about them. However, referring to the Action Notebook each day is like developing any other new habit. Someone once said, "Habit, unlike instinct, must be acquired by practice."

The Action Notebook replaces the **PENDING** Box used during the Centralizing Step. It eliminates papers piling up on the counter tops and smothering the refrigerator door. The Action Notebook can serve as a memory bank for you that will save you time, money, and a lot of frustration. When my daughters and I return from the public library, for example, we immediately remove the cards from the books. I put a rubber band around the pack of cards and file it in the Action Notebook behind the date the books are due. When the books need to be returned to the library, the cards are repocketed. If there are any leftover cards, the little search party knows exactly which missing titles need to be located.

No longer do calendars need to be crammed with important pending papers until the bindings gasp and give up the ghost. Whenever a piece of paper accompanies a date on the calendar, file it in the Action Notebook until it is needed.

The dilemma of papers getting buried or lost in the shuffle until the deadline expires is a problem of the past. In fact, the only bad part about an Action Notebook is that it leaves absolutely no excuse to miss anybody's birthday.

Mail

One day while visiting a friend, I observed her opening the mail. After peeking at the contents of each bill and letter, she shoved the papers back into the envelopes. Then she stuffed the whole works into a cubbyhole on her kitchen counter along with, it seemed, a week's worth of mail.

Another acquaintance handles his mail in a totally different manner. He doesn't exactly ignore it, but almost. When he receives his mail, he sorts it. If the item is a bill or personal letter, he tosses it into one box. Everything else goes into a second box. At the end of the month, he sifts through the first box, pays the bills, and reads the letter. Once a year, maybe, he gets around to the second box.

When, where, and how do you handle *your* personal mail? Let's discuss these issues one at a time.

When?

Sometimes it is impossible to read the mail when it is received. That can be frustrating if the highlight of the day is opening the mailbox. If you're cooking spaghetti sauce, setting the table and checking on your child's day at school, however, don't attempt to digest a letter informing you your car insurance has been canceled. If you are unable to read your mail when you receive it, put it on your desk until later. When you can give the mail your undivided attention, you will be able to effectively carry out the three How Steps outlined below.

Where?

I don't feel it matters too much *where* the mail is read, as long as the three How Steps are followed. Some days I enjoy sitting on my davenport with the warm sun shining on me to read my mail. Other days, I sit at the kitchen table or at my desk in my office. I like the flexibility. The important issue in handling the mail is not when or where, but *how*.

How?

Office secretaries process an impressive amount of mail each year. The methods they use to efficiently handle incoming and outgoing mail are more detailed than are needed for the average personal mail load. However, three basic steps gleaned from their procedures, as well as some helpful tips, can be used to handle mail on the homefront.

Step 1. *Opening the Mail.* The first step in handling the mail is to open it. Sound simple? Don't forget my friend with the two boxes. Actually, *not* opening the mail is a part of this step, too. When you read your mail, decide whether or not you want to open it. Don't waste the time opening an envelope if it's an advertisement for a product or service you don't want, don't need, or can't afford.

Use a letter opener for the mail you do open. It eliminates the chance of tearing the contents. After you open the envelope, date or date-stamp the correspondence if it isn't already dated. You will not regret this habit.

Step 2. *Sorting the Mail.* Time management consultants emphasize the importance of handling a piece of paper only once. I agree — to a degree. I don't believe it is always possible. Sometimes it's a matter of money or time that causes papers to be shuffled several times. If I don't have the money, for instance, I may have to wait a week to act on an offer for theater tickets. If I don't have the time, a letter may not receive an answer for a month until I can gather information to properly respond. Sometimes people handle a piece of paper two or three times out of sheer joy, as when one receives a long-awaited check in the mail; or out of pure anger, as when one receives a check that turns out bad.

My friend who stashes her weekly mail on the kitchen counter, however, can minimize handling her paperwork if she confronts it as she opens the mail. The second step in handling the mail is to sort it.

As you read your mail, divide it into these three categories:

1. **Personal Business Correspondence,** including: bills, bank statements, notices concerning the house, coupons, and advertisements.

2. **Personal Correspondence,** including: letters and notes, invitations, cards, genealogical research replies, and magazines.

3. **Garbage,** including: junk mail, irrelevant correspondence, envelopes, and unwanted enclosures.

If you have a business in your home, your mail will include a fourth category:

4. **Professional Correspondence,** including: bills, bank statements, transactions, advertising, and magazines.

Step 3. *Distributing the Mail.* The third step in handling the mail is to distribute it. If the mail is read at a desk, appropriate files are accessible for storing the paperwork. Since I enjoy reading my mail in different locations, however, sometimes extra physical effort is necessary to file it. I'm willing to sacrifice the convenience of opening the mail at my desk. There is no comparison to reading a letter over a lemonade at my picnic table under the old willow tree.

Whenever you read your mail, once it is opened and sorted, use the following three "tools" to distribute it:

1. **The Action Notebook(s)** - Personal and Professional (if applicable).

   a. **Personal Business Correspondence** to be acted upon is filed in the Action Notebook. A bill usually includes advertising flyers. Unless they are of a particular interest to you, throw away the extra enclosures. File the statement and its return envelope in the Action Notebook behind the appropriate date. Bank statements can be filed in the front or "A" pocket of the Action Notebook. Determine what action is needed on notices concerning the house and file them accordingly, for example, property tax statement, salt delivery schedule for water softener, and such.

b. **Personal Correspondence** can be divided into three areas:

1. *To be answered immediately* - file these letters in the "A" pocket of the Action Notebook.

2. *To be answered sometime* - file these letters in a special Personal Correspondence Center (see section in this chapter).

3. *Answered* - either throw the letter received away or, if you want to save it, file it in the **PERSONAL CORRESPONDENCE FILE** (see later).

c. **Professional Business Correspondence** to be acted upon is filed in its own Action Notebook.

2. **The Prefiling Boxes or Folders**
Some mail does not require any action and can be filed in established files. If you don't have time to file papers immediately, determine which category is appropriate and put the items in an interim location to be filed later. Prefiling boxes or folders are discussed in Chapter Ten.

3. **The Wastebasket**
The most popular "tool" in handling the mail should be the wastebasket. I know a woman who sorts her mail by the wastebasket as she removes it from her post office box. She keeps what she wants and lets the post office throw away her garbage. Learn to evaluate immediately as you read your mail and discard items that have little or no significance. Use the Ten Criteria questions outlined in Chapter One to help you decide whether or not to keep a piece of mail. Generally, you should end up with more trash to throw away than papers to act upon or to file.

Mail Tips

1. Whenever possible, **respond to a letter immediately.** The longer you postpone answering, the more lengthy the response needs to be.

2. **Reply on the original letter.** If you need to keep the original letter, use the back of it on which to type your carbon copy. It saves time, money and space in your files.

3. When you open the mail, **always double check the return address.**
   Make sure it is on the letter before you discard the envelope. If there
   is a change, indicate it in your Rolodex (see section on Rolodex in
   this chapter).

4. **Check the envelope for enclosures** when opening the mail. Make
   sure everything is included that the letter indicates.

Personal Correspondence Center

How do you feel when you unexpectedly receive a card or note in the
mail? It's a pleasant feeling, isn't it? Many people claim the following
reasons prevent them from being thoughtful: disorganization, lack of
time, too many people expecting letters, cost of postage.

The dilemma of disorganization can be solved by creating a Personal
Correspondence Center. It can be a designated corner of a desk, an old
picnic basket, or even a garden tool tote box. I enameled an old desk
with bright yellow paint and christened it my Personal Correspondence
Center. Stock the center with the following supplies:

Stamps (for letters and postcards)   Carbon paper
Stationery   Stapler, staples, staple remover
Stationery note cards
Post cards
Greeting cards (see section on Greeting Cards in this chapter)
Envelopes
Supply of gummed return labels (or rubber stamp)
Pens (ballpoint and/or fine-tip felt pens)
Transparent tape
Scissors

In the center, I also keep an active supply of favorite cartoons and fun
quips I enjoy including in my letters.

Since the Action Notebook is referred to every day, letters "to be
answered immediately" are filed in
it. Keep other personal correspondence that can be answered any
time in the Personal Correspondence Center. If you use a desk
that doesn't have partitions, a
vertical letter sorter can be used to
organize current correspondence.
If your center is a garden tool tote
box, specify one section for letters
to be answered.

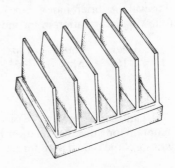

It is as much fun to review old letters as it is to send them. If you want to save personal letters that have been answered, establish a **PERSONAL CORRESPONDENCE FILE** using the PREFIX METHOD.

The File…Don't Pile™ Paperdex™

PC
Pers. Corres.

SUBJECT	SEE ALSO	SEE
PC101-Family		
PC102-Priscilla		
PC103-Bev		
PC104-Nan		
PC105-Minnesota		
PC106-Wisconsin		
PC107-Iowa		
PC108-Misc. U.S.		
PC109-Foreign		
PC110-Missing		

If you regularly receive correspondence from certain people, assign separate folders for their letters. If you hear from some individuals on an infrequent basis, lump them geographically, for instance, Iowa. Missing friends are simply that, missing. For instance, I have the letter I received from a friend plus the letter I sent to her, which was returned to me marked "address unknown." I could throw both letters away, but then I would have nothing — and I really want to track her down.

If you have special letters you don't want to keep in file folders, mount them in scrapbooks. Use plastic pages so both sides of the letter can be read. I have my Grandmother's letters filed in chronological order in this form. If you have too many letters from an individual to fit into a file folder, they can be tied with a pretty ribbon and kept in a shoebox. Number each envelope in the upper right corner for faster retrieval. A brief index can be kept on the shoebox lid. Cite the following information in the index for each letter:

No.	Day	Month	Year	To	Location
1	16	May	1963	Sallie Heise	New London, Wis.

	From	Location
	Pat Morack	Oshkosh, Wis.

Organizing a Personal Correspondence Center makes it easier to maintain long distance relationships. As Lord Byron once said, "Letter-writing is the only device for combining solitude and good company."

Greeting Cards

"When you care enough to send the very best" is the motto of a major greeting card company. It is often the case, however, that a card needed in a hurry is purchased in a flurry. A card might be found, but the motto sounds more like, "When you only have time enough to send the very least."

There is a right way to organize greeting cards so you'll have the right card on hand when it is needed. Stationery stores, as well as Current Products, Inc. (Colorado Springs, CO 80941), offer compact reminder books for birthdays, anniversaries, and other special days. The monthly pages in the books have pockets in which to store cards. Each pocket page has lines for the days of the month on which to note friends' and relatives' names and the special occasions. The advantage of the book is that it provides a place to store cards well in advance of events. For example, if a fun and fitting card for cousin Chris is purchased in May and her birthday isn't until December, the card is filed in the December pocket until it is needed.

A **GREETING CARD FILE** can be established to store cards for general use. If the **PERSONAL CORRESPONDENCE FILE INDEX** only uses the top half of a Paperdex sheet, use the bottom half of the sheet for the **GREETING CARD FILE INDEX**. The file folders for both mini-categories can be stored in a small tote box near the Personal Correspondence Center. Use distinctive colors such as blue and red to mark the codes on the tabs, as the two categories are filed in the same box or drawer.

GREETING CARD INDEX
GC101 - Birthday
GC102 - Baby
GC103 - Get Well
GC104 - Thank You
GC105 - Friendship/Hello/Good-bye
GC106 - Anniversary
GC107 - Sympathy
GC108 - Future Use
GC109 - Back & Forth
GC110 - Postcards
GC111 - Misc.

A card filed in the *Future Use* folder is an example of how Criteria Question Five, "Do you foresee a use for it?" can be answered. "Yes!" One day as I browsed through a card shop, I spied the perfect birthday card for my daughter Molly who has a thimble collection. It reads, "For being such a special daughter, here's a genuine, imported solid gold THIMBLE ... it's a kind of Status Thimble! (Like having you for a daughter.)" (American Greeting Card Company.) Molly is a little young to appreciate it now, so the card has to be saved for future use. I know a person who found a birthday card for someone celebrating a 50th birthday. She wants to spring it on her sister, who is forty. Now *that's* planning ahead!

Back and Forth cards are cards that are usually signed, "Guess Who!" or "Me!" They are mailed back and forth over many years and become a standing joke. *Back and forth* cards can foster a spark in a relationship that lasts long after the cards fall apart.

The *Post Cards* folder can include fun and silly cards, lovely ones purchased at the art museum or the local scenic type. Sometimes in February I send a beautiful snow scene of Minneapolis to a friend in California and sign it simply, "Wish you were here!" Some winters I send an oceanside scene of California to the same friend and sign it, "Wish I were *there!*"

The **PERSONAL CORRESPON-DENCE FILE** and the **GREETING CARD FILE** can be stored in the same drawer. The reminder book of greeting cards can be stored in front of the **GREETING CARD FILE INDEX.** At the beginning of each month, remove cards to be sent that month to specific people. Address the cards, stamp them, and file them behind the appropriate dates in the Action Notebook. The **GREETING CARD FILE** can be replenished as needed. Watch for special sales and stores going out of business. The time to stock up on cards is when they're selling at a 50 percent to 75 percent discount. It saves time and money.

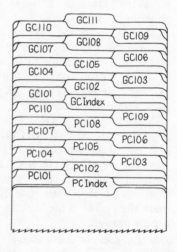

While it is uplifting to be remembered, it is as much fun to be thoughtful. Sending thoughtful cards and notes to friends and relatives at the right time is easier when there is a ready supply.

Rolodex

One product on the market for years prevails in every office, but is often overlooked for home use. It is the desk top card file. Different companies offer a variety of styles of desk top card files. All types serve the purpose of providing an efficient unit for filing names, addresses, and information. For simplification, this discussion uses the term Rolodex, a brand name.

A Rolodex is available in a plastic frame in various sizes, 2¼" x 4", 3" x 5", 4" x 6", and 5" x 8". It usually has a 500 to 1000 card capacity.

Each unit comes with a supply of cards and one set of alphabetical guides made of heavy acetate. The cards are easy to remove and snap into place after data is added. There is no worry about cards falling out or getting lost.

Here are some ways addresses and phone numbers can be filed in a Rolodex for home use:

1. ADDRESS LIST

The alphabetical guides can be used in the first section of the Rolodex. This section can be an address list of personal friends, if you wish, or an organization's membership list or whatever you prefer. I use this section in my Rolodex as a church directory. When people move in and out of the congregation, it is difficult to keep a directory in book form neat and up-to-date. I photocopy the pages of the most recent edition of the directory the church furnishes. Then I cut the names of the families apart from the book and tape the information on cards, one family per card. By using a Rolodex, a card can be easily removed if a family moves, or added if a new family moves in. If I want to maintain contact with a person who moves, I change the address on the card and file it in another section of the Rolodex.

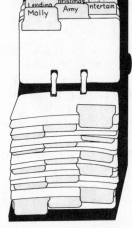

2. SUBJECT HEADINGS

Purchase a package of pressure-sensitive celluloid index tabs in assorted colors at an office supply store. Create subject headings pertinent to your needs. Attach an index tab to a blank card, insert the subject heading and file the guide in the Rolodex. File information behind the guide relevant to that section. For example:

a. "Yellow Pages"
This section includes information concerning businesses and services you frequently use. Instead of tacking lists and bits of papers with phone

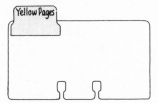

numbers by the telephone, put the information on cards and file them in a Rolodex. There is no need to continually transfer numbers every time you receive a new phone book if you use the Rolodex. A "Yellow Pages" section might include the following:

American Automobile Association	— telephone numbers
Bank	— numbers and hours
Beauty shop	— number
Dogcatcher	— number
Garbage service	— number
Handyman or repair services	— numbers
(e.g., car repair shop; plumber)	
Health center	— number
	doctors' names
Insurance agents	— numbers
Newspapers	
Carriers	— numbers
Circulation offices	— numbers
Pharmacy	— numbers and hours
Post office	— number and hours
Public information services	— numbers
(e.g., road conditions for winter driving)	
Restaurants	— numbers and hours
(e.g., pizza parlor for takeouts)	
School offices	— numbers
	teachers' names
Stores	— numbers for each
	branch
	hours

Tape business cards onto Rolodex cards and file. This is why I prefer the 3″ x 5″ sized Rolodex. Tape short 2″ x 4″ newspaper articles onto cards for services such as, "Free Gardening Advice at Ag. Extn. Service." The article provides the telephone number, hours, and what information is available.

File the cards within the "Yellow Pages" section alphabetically as you would think of them. If you would think of *Plumber* instead of *Nelson, John,* file it under *Plumber.* Use a yellow-colored index tab for the guide to this section.

b. Babysitters.

File names of sitters alphabetically within this section.

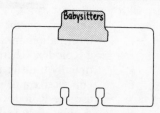

c. Neighbors.
File names of neighbors alphabetically within this section. Include address, phone number, and description of their residence as well as its location in relation to your residence.

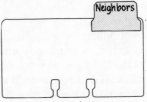

This information is valuable in an emergency for babysitters or guests in your home who might not be familiar with your neighborhood.

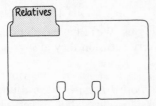

d. Relatives
File names of relatives alphabetically within this section. Include addresses, phone numbers, and their relationship to you. This information is especially valuable if you live alone and have no immediate relatives living in the area. In an emergency, others would know how to reach your family.

e. Friends (Local)

f. Friends (Out-of-Town)
File names of friends alphabetically within each of these sections. Include addresses, telephone numbers, and other information such as birthdays.

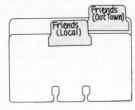

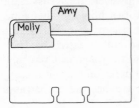

g. Children's Friends
File names of your children's friends alphabetically, usually by first name, within this section. Molly and Amy enjoy printing and filing their own cards.

h. Christmas or Hanukkah List
File names alphabetically within this section of those to whom you send cards. Include addresses and date cards were sent if desired.

The function of a home Rolodex extends far beyond an address list. Here are more examples of how a Rolodex can help in home organization.

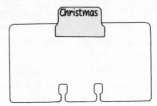

i. Entertaining

This section can be considered the *To Whom I Fed What* department. If you entertain frequently and want to remember what you fed your guests the last time they visited, note the menu on a card with their names. File guests' names alphabetically within this section. A woman in my workshop shared this experience she and her husband had when they visited her parents. Her husband said,  "your folks must not have been expecting us. We're having chicken." She realized for the first time that on every occasion they always had roast beef.

j. Lending

This section can be considered the *To Whom I Loaned What* department. If you often loan items or books to others, but forget who borrowed them, note this information, including the date loaned, on a card with the borrower's name. File the card within this section alphabetically either by the name of the borrower or the item. The borrower doesn't need to know you're keeping a record. On the other hand, sometimes it might be an excellent idea to let them know you are! Be sure your identification is on the item or book being borrowed also.

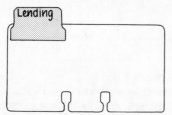 Sometimes feelings are hurt when borrowed items are kept an undue length of time. In today's fast-paced lifestyle, however, it is easy to innocently forget how long items have been kept. In many cases, the borrower is so embarrassed, he doesn't know how to graciously return the item. By keeping a record in the Rolodex of items on loan, it is easy to provide a gentle reminder before the loan reaches the embarrassing stage.

k. Borrowing

This section is the reverse of the Lending section. It can be considered the *From Whom I Borrowed What* department. If you borrow items or books from others, but tend to forget what you borrow from whom, note the information including the date borrowed on a card with the lender's name. File the card alphabetically within this section, either according to the name of the lender or the item borrowed.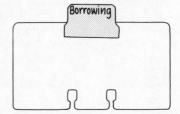

Information filed in this section saves frustration and hard feelings. Titles of books borrowed from the public library should be kept in the Action Notebook described earlier in this chapter since the books have specified due dates.

l. Location
This section can be considered the *Where I Put What* department. Do you sometimes put items in a box in the garage or basement and forget where you put them? Note the information on a card, including a description of the box if necessary. File the card alphabetically within this section according to the item. In Chapter Six the REMINDER cross reference illustrates a method of 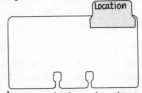 noting items too big to fit into file folders, such as Halloween decorations. Such REMINDER cross references are not advisable, however, if you move a lot. Your new home may not have a cupboard beneath the basement steps to store the Halloween box. Note the location of items on cards and file them alphabetically within this section according to the item.

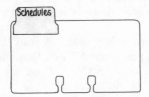

m. Schedules
If a Schedule Section is not kept in an Action Notebook, this information can be filed in the Rolodex. Schedules can range from housecleaning to piano lessons, school vacations to football practice. This section does not replace calendars or "to do" lists. It can serve, however, as a yearly master list of events.

The Rolodex is a versatile tool to use in home organization. Subject headings vary according to individual needs and interests. The Rolodex has been referred to as an inexpensive version of the home computer. Let it be your memory. If you feel you can't afford a Rolodex, ask for one for your birthday. You'll love it!

3. ON-THE-ROAD ADDRESS BOOK
The Rolodex is great to have on the desk at home. But what happens if you need an address and phone number when you're on the road? Small address ring binders with A-Z index tabs and replaceable page forms are handy substitutes for a Rolodex. One name, address, and phone number can be recorded on a form. The book is easy to keep in order and up to date. The forms and books come in various sizes and are available at most office supply stores.

4. HOME BUSINESS ROLODEX

If you own a business in your home, either have a separate Rolodex for networking contacts and clients, or create a BUSINESS section within your personal Rolodex.

Newspapers and Magazines

The real fun in having the File ... Don't Pile system established comes to light when the morning newspaper or a new magazine arrives in the mail. A kind of glazed look comes over your eyes as you clip articles and ads. You can't help but smile because you know precisely where each item will be filed. Here are some helpful tips for clipping newspapers and magazines.

Newspapers

Unless someone behind you wants to read the newspaper, read it with a scissors in hand. Or use handy gadgets to remove articles, such as a Clipit paper cutter or a seam ripper. They are compact precision instruments and have safety caps for protection. Another safe clipper is the Krazy Cutter which cuts through the top sheet only of a magazine or newspaper. (A&W Products Co., Port Jervis, NY 12771.) Clip the articles, ads, or coupons immediately. You won't have to retrace your steps to locate the items. That often proves to be a needle-in-the-haystack experience.

If you can't cut information out because others want to read the newspaper, too, read with a bright-colored pen in hand. Circle the items or mark them with an "x." Even note the word "SAVE," if you wish. When you can clip them, locating the articles will be easier.

Do you want to preserve old newspaper clippings that are turning yellow and threatening to crumble? Experts at the National Archives suggest the following method:

1. Mix 1 teaspoon of magnesium carbonate and a quart of club soda in a large plastic dish.

2. Sandwich the clippings between two pieces of screen or Pellon, a material sold in most fabric stores. Soak for thirty minutes.

3. Mop up excess liquid with blotting paper and allow to dry overnight on more blotting paper.

4. Store clippings in a well-sealed flat plastic bag. They should keep forever.

Magazines

One of my clients admitted that her back issues of magazines reached the Leaning Tower of Pisa stage. She said, "I hate to miss buying my favorite magazines. But I have a tendency to buy them and not read

them entirely. I tell myself, 'I'll save this and read it later. Then I'll decide if there's something worth cutting out and saving.'"

My closet used to lean to the left for the same reason, but I experienced an added dilemma. I attempted clipping my magazines, but always felt stymied when I wanted articles that ran back to back. I didn't know how to solve the problem short of buying two subscriptions or photocopying half the magazine.

Then one day I discovered the answer. It involves three steps. To demonstrate, using a *Reader's Digest* and two articles that, on some pages, run back to back, here are the three steps to follow:

Article 1 - "The Day Mother Cried" by Gerald Moore

Article 2 - "Would a Wood Stove Work for You?" by Dorothy Gow Stroetzel

Step 1. Remove the first article, "The Day Mother Cried" (a story about courage). It will include a page of the second article on the back. Staple the pages together. Date and source it, for example, Sept. 1980, *Reader's Digest*. Code it, specifically, C104 (the code for courage). Set it aside.

Step 2. Remove the remaining pages of the second article, "Would a Wood Stove Work for You?" (energy saving information). Staple the pages together. Date and source it, for example, Sept. 1980, *Reader's Digest*. Code it, specifically, E102 (the code for energy). Indicate the title of the article at the top of the page since this is not the first page of the article. Note in the margin where the beginning of the article can be found, specifically, "For the beginning of this article, see C104 Religion File on back of 'The Day Mother Cried.'"

Step 3. Turn the first article over so the first page of the second article appears. On the bottom of the page note where the remainder of the article can be found, specifically, "For the rest of this article, see E102 Home Mgt. File."

When articles are filed in two different categories, be sure to include the category with the code in your notations. It is possible to go through a whole magazine like dominoes, if you use this method to clip articles that run back to back.

Photocopying might still be necessary in some cases. For example, one side of a magazine page might be the conclusion of an article about roses. The reverse side might be several miscellaneous gardening tips on a variety of subjects. If both sides are wanted, it is worth the nickel to photocopy the tips so they can be clipped and filed under the appropriate subjects.

When reading a magazine, develop the habit of reading it with either a scissors or a felt tip pen in hand. If you can't clip the articles as you read them, note on the cover of the magazine which pages you want to save. This prevents wasting time searching through magazines for information you thought you would never forget. One workshop participant uses this system when she reads her magazines:

1st - After she buys the magazine she glances through it.

2nd - The second time she picks up the magazine, she reads it more seriously, dog-earring pages she thinks she might want to save.

3rd - She reviews the magazine a third time and removes any of the dog-earred pages she really feels are worthwhile.

4th - She tears the cover in half to indicate she is finished and tosses it.

This involves handling a piece of paper more times than recommended by time management consultants, but she is systematic and realistic in her approach in dealing with her magazines. They don't pile up.

Coupons

There are three types of coupon clippers. The first type voraciously rips coupons out of magazines and newspapers, "files" them in her purse or pocket, and forgets them until they surface three weeks after the deadline.

The second type conscientiously highlights expiration dates with a bright pen, files the coupons in envelopes and even takes them to the store, but forgets to give them to the checkout clerk.

The third type is both voracious and conscientious. Not only are coupons clipped, highlighted, and filed, but so are labels, box tops, seals, wrappers, and proofs of purchase. Some actually use them, some don't.

Whatever the degree of interest you have in accumulating coupons, the bottom line is: Do you control and use them, or do they control and use you?

Storing Coupons

There are several organizers on the market that would be helpful for the first two types to store coupons. One kind of organizer is in wallet form. Separate pockets and self-stick labels for categories are provided. Another device is a 4″ x 6″ recipe box organizer with product dividers. Some boxes even come with a supply of coupons. Still a third kind of organizer is in book form with pockets on each page in which to store coupons.

A homemade version is a child's shoebox with envelopes designated for different categories of products. Categories vary according to individual and family needs and tastes. Here are some suggestions:

Baby Products	Delicatessen
Bakery Goods	Desserts
Baking Supplies	Frozen Foods
Beverages	Health/Beauty Aids
Breakfast Foods/Cereals	Meats
Canned Fruit/Vegetables	Pet Foods/Supplies
Cleaning Products/Paper	Prepared Foods
Condiments/Dressings	Produce
Dairy	Soups/Sauces

The third type of coupon clipper usually has a bigger supply of coupons to organize. Some of these clippers can be considered hardcore refunders. A woman who teaches classes on refunding attended a File ... Don't Pile workshop. She now uses the A-Z METHOD to file her accumulation. She is able to retrieve any tuna label, coupon, proof of purchase, you name it. Two books on refunding offer suggestions on filing coupons: *Ask the Coupon Queen,* by Mary Ann Hayes, and *Cashing in at the Checkout,* by Susan J. Samtur.

Using Coupons

Of what value are boxes of coupons, if they aren't used? The wallet and book forms of organizers make it easier to carry coupons to the store. But you have to develop the habit of using them. Some shoppers take a small shoebox of coupons with them to the store and place it in the children's seat of the grocery cart. If a special is being offered for a specific brand of catsup, they can cash in on the savings because they have all of the catsup coupons on hand.

Here is a three-step plan that not only helps in using coupons, but saves shopping time and money as well.

Step 1. Draw map of store and list products.

A. Make a trip to your favorite grocery store with:

1. A full stomach
2. A clipboard holding 8½" x 11" paper
3. A pencil
4. No children
5. Plenty of time

B. Draw a map of the store including:

1. Lists of products you normally buy that are shelved in each aisle.
2. Other information of interest, i.e., bathroom, water fountain.

The purpose of this step is to "case the joint," not to go grocery shopping. However, you might at least buy a pack of gum and smile at the manager on your way out the door.

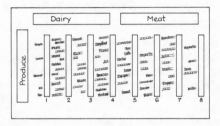

Step 2.   Redraw map and make master list.

A. Neatly redraw the map on another piece of 8½″ x 11″ paper. Do not include the lists or products on this second map.

B. Type an Aisle Directory on a separate piece of paper. List the items noted on the first map.

For example:

AISLE DIRECTORY

Aisle 1	*Aisle 2*	*Aisle 3*
Mayonnaise	Jam	Canned Meats
Dressings	Peanut Butter	Canned Fish
Canned Fruits	Pickles, Olives	Powdered Milk
Fruit Juices	Canned Vegetables	Soup
Catsup	Vinegar	Pasta

The purpose of this step is to develop a master list of the products you normally buy and their location in the store. Store managers sometimes move products to new locations for marketing reasons, but generally the layout of the store remains constant.

Step 3.   Reproduce supply of grocery list maps.

A. Have a small supply of map 2 photocopied or printed at an instant print shop.

B. File the supply of maps and the Aisle Directory in a logical category, for example, **MONEY MANAGEMENT FILE.**

The purpose of this step is to create a supply of forms on which you can write your weekly or monthly grocery list. Some grocery stores furnish directories, but they are not as personalized or handy as the one you create. Here's how you can use your map and directory to help you use your coupons and save time and money shopping.

1. *Plan a weekly or monthly menu.*
   Menu plans don't need to be so structured they can't be changed. Plans help you to have meal ideas in mind and allow you to be more imaginative. Use store ads to take advantage of food bargains when you plan your menus.

2. *Write items needed on the grocery list map.*
   Using the Aisle Directory as a guide, list items needed for the menus on your map. Be flexible to allow for extra items for unexpected guests. Some people keep maps handy so they can add items as they get low.

3. *Locate coupons for items on grocery list map.*
   Fold map outward in half (like a mini-file folder), and slip inside an envelope of coupons needed for the list.

4. *Go shopping! (Eat first.)*
   Whip out the map, buzz down the aisles, and put the needed items in your grocery cart. If no items are listed in Aisle 2 on the map, don't go down Aisle 2. When you finish, you'll have coupons in hand to give to the checkout clerk.

   The grocery list map is a handy method when others need to shop for you. If they aren't as familiar with the store as you are, the map makes the shopping trip go smoother and faster.

   Before the sun rises tomorrow, clean off the refrigerator and clear off the counter tops. Start today to follow the steps in this chapter. You will have a happier way of getting through the day.

Summary

Action Notebook

1. File "must do" papers in front pocket of notebook.
2. File "should do" papers in index sections 1-31 and/or January-December.
3. File "could do" papers in back pocket of notebook.
4. Add sections such as **Spouse, Schedules,** or **Sunday** as needed.

Mail

Step 1. Open.   Step 2. Sort.   Step 3. Distribute.

Greeting Cards

1. Use reminder books to store cards, or
2. Use **GREETING CARD FILE** to store cards.

Rolodex

1. Address List
2. Subject Headings
   a. Yellow Pages
   b. Babysitters
   c. Neighbors
   d. Relatives
   e. Friends (local)
   f. Friends (out-of-town)
   g. Children's Friends
   h. Christmas or Hanukkah List
   i. Entertaining
   j. Lending
   k. Borrowing
   l. Location
   m. Schedules
3. On-the-Road Address Book
4. Home Business Rolodex

Newspapers and Magazines

1. If possible, clip information immediately.
2. If impossible to clip immediately, circle information with pen.
3. Use three-step system to clip back-to-back magazine articles.

Coupons

1. Storing: wallets, books, boxes, envelopes, and the A-Z METHOD.
2. Using:

Step 1 Draw map of store and list products.

Step 2 Redraw map and make master list.

Step 3 Reproduce supply of grocery list maps.
       Attach coupons to map and go shopping.

Chapter Nine
Do You Have Your Receipt?

Disasters Happen Only to Others

Picture yourself coming home from a restful vacation. It's great to be home. As you turn into your driveway, however, your happy mood suddenly changes. The charred framework is almost all that remains of your lovely home. Gone are the record collection, the just-cleaned carpeting, the closet filled with new ski clothes, and the memories mounted in photo albums. Gone, too, are the important papers to substantiate your losses.

Having a home destroyed by fire or a tornado is something that happens only to someone else. That's what most people want to believe. But, it *can* happen to you. Every day more than 2,000 homes are burned in the United States. Tornadoes, floods, and other disasters "kill hundreds of Americans every year, injure thousands, inflict widespread suffering and hardship, and cause great economic loss." (*In Time of Emergency,* by the Office of Civil Defense.) If your home were destroyed today, would you be able to present a household inventory complete with receipts and photos to your insurance agent? In 1984, nearly three million homes were burglarized or robbed in the United States. Stop and think. Are your valuables in a safe place this minute?

An itemized record of household goods is merely one aspect of a **PERSONAL BUSINESS FILE.** Take this short quiz. Where would you look for answers to these questions:

1. You are selling your home. You made substantial improvements in your home. Can you prove it?

2. You have just lost your wallet. The $100 wasn't so important, but the papers in it were. What papers were in it?

141

3. You are registering your child for school. Can you verify her birthdate and immunizations?

Could you answer the questions in sixty seconds or less? This chapter discusses many kinds of papers that affect one's personal business.

Personal Business File

Although mention was made in Chapter Five, it is important to restate how a **PERSONAL BUSINESS FILE** differs from a **MONEY MANAGEMENT FILE**. A **MONEY MANAGEMENT FILE** includes money-related articles for reference, such as, *how* to buy insurance. On the other hand, a **PERSONAL BUSINESS FILE** includes personally related papers for documentation, such as an insurance policy. *The purpose of a* **PERSONAL BUSINESS FILE** *is to document.*

There are three concerns people have in dealing with personal business papers.

1. *Where* should the papers be stored?

2. *What* papers need to be retained?

3. *How long* should the papers be retained?

In a Safe Place

Determining where to store personal business papers is an individual decision. Whatever location you select for protecting your valuable papers, the important issue is that original documents should be kept in a safe place. Copies of the originals can be kept in a file cabinet, desk drawer, or tote box. Some of the most commonly used storage locations for original documents are:

1. *A Fire Resistant Box*

Many people consider a metal box fireproof. A better description of a metal box would be an incinerator. In order for a metal box to be labeled fire resistant, it must be tested by Underwriters Laboratories and be insulated with asbestos. Such a box might be better protection for papers than a suitcase, but it isn't much protection from a thief. The only advantage of having a small metal box is that it provides quick removal in an emergency. That depends, of course, if the box is stored in a handy location and if there is time to retrieve it. One woman I interviewed said she was grateful to have gotten her three sons out of their burning home. When she was told the house was going to blow, there wasn't any thought of going back in, not even for a metal box.

2. *Home Safe*

Many homeowners store their important records in a home safe. Generally, it is compact, convenient, and fire resistant. If tax records are kept in the safe, the cost of the safe is tax deductible. Many decorative cabinets and covers can be purchased to conceal a safe and can serve as furniture also. In apartments where space is limited, this is an added benefit.

It's important to understand the distinction between a fire resistant and a burglar resistant home safe. All home safes tested by Underwriters Laboratories are fire resistant. The safes are rated for one, two, or four hours in conditions simulating a 1700 degree fire. It is not until a home safe weighs at least 750 pounds, however, that it is also considered burglar resistant. Naturally, the heavier the safe, the more expensive it becomes. Although the small fire safe is no protection against burglary or forcible entry, it can cause an intruder enough inconvenience to reconsider his/her actions. According to a safe expert, the average amateur thief realizes the risks and wants to be in and out of a house in ten minutes. If a safe is bolted to the floor, it is generally passed by for more easily removed items.

The least expensive safe that is both fire and burglar resistant is a floor safe. It is a unique cylinder which comes in a variety of sizes ranging from one to two and a half feet deep. Once the safe is installed into a basement floor, it is flush with the concrete and can be hidden under carpeting. It is virtually undetectable.

3. *Safe Deposit Box*

Perhaps the most widely-used location for storing valuable papers and small items is a safe deposit box. Safe deposit boxes are available at banks for a small annual rental fee. Some savings institutions provide boxes free to depositors. Many families find the smallest-sized box adequate for their needs, although larger boxes are available. Safe deposit boxes are housed in a highly secure location of the bank. An employee of the bank cannot open a box alone since both your key and a key from the bank are required. Neither one alone can open it. If anyone tried to open your box, he/she would need to forge your signature under the watchful eye of the bank employee responsible for safe deposit boxes. Some institutions also take photos of the person opening the box. If you lose your key, the customer side of the lock must be drilled out by a locksmith. The law requires that either the customer and one bank officer or two bank officers be present at the time the lock is drilled. A third bank officer notarizes the witnesses.

The main disadvantages of a safe deposit box are the two access restrictions. First, you are limited to bank hours. Second, the box is sealed by law upon the death of the owner. A bank employee is assigned the duty of checking daily obituaries to see if any renters are listed. The first person to check the contents of the box is a state tax official. Even a co-renter cannot get into the box to get deeds to property he or she owns. Survivors cannot have possession of items left in the box until the will is probated. This may take a month or, if the will is contested, even five years or more. If valuables or cash are found in the box, tax officials assume they belong to the deceased.

4. *Safe Deposit Vault*
Another location in which people store valuable belongings is a commercially operated safe deposit vault. Such vaults are popping up in shopping malls throughout the country. The advantages of this option are the unrestrictive accessibility and the size availability of the boxes. The smallest-sized box in a vault store is generally the largest size available in a bank. The disadvantage of this commercial-type deposit box is the cost.

It was not tongue-in-cheek when I mentioned at the beginning of Chapter Eight that many freezers contain vital papers. Many people store original documents in the freezer compartment above the refrigerator, believing the papers are safe from a fire. A refrigerator is fire resistant to some extent because heat has difficulty penetrating the space created in the freezer walls. But if the refrigerator falls through the floor and the door pops open, the papers would be destroyed. The major reason a fire safe has a combination lock is not to make it burglar resistant. The lock is merely to prevent the safe door from opening during the drop test by Underwriters Laboratories. During the test, a fire-damaged safe is dropped thirty feet. If the door opens on impact, the safe fails. A freezer is a prime target for a burglar. (Although it seems to me at today's prices, a thief wouldn't bother with a pile of papers. He'd take the meat!) A freezer is better than two other storage options I've encountered, however — a galvanized garbage can and under the mattress.

Pending Personal Business Papers

A **PERSONAL BUSINESS FILE** includes two types of papers. One type is pending or those papers requiring action. Personal business papers considered pending include:

1. *Monthly unpaid bills, new and ongoing*
These papers are filed behind the appropriate date in the Action

Notebook. (See Chapter Eight.) When bills are paid, where and how long do statement stubs need to be kept? The answers depend on your purpose in keeping the stubs in the first place.

If your purpose is . . .

to prove the bills are paid . . . The stubs are proof of cash payment; otherwise, canceled checks are. Throw stubs away.

to draw a comparison with previous year's bills . . . Record information in a ledger. It involves less space and loose papers. Or call the utility company for figures; it has data on computer. Throw stubs away.

to prove a tax deduction . . . File stubs with current tax papers.

to feel secure . . . Store in expandable receipt file for one or two years. Beyond that is not security; it's sentimental. Throw stubs away.

People file stubs year after year and don't throw them away unless they move. Some people keep a triple record of their bills, specifically, stubs, canceled checks, and a ledger. This is redundant and time consuming.

2. *Unpaid sales receipts*

Tissue copies of credit card transactions can be filed in an expandable receipt file in appropriately marked envelopes. Throw receipts away after charges are matched against the monthly statement. If an item that has been charged needs to be returned, the store computer has a record of the transaction. If an item was purchased with cash, sales

| VISA |
| Sears |
| Mobil |
| JC Penneys |

| March |
| February |
| January |
| Blue sweater |
| Wool slacks |
| Down coat |
| Scarf |
| Mittens |
| Swim suit for Florida trip |

receipts can be filed either in an expandable receipt file or in 9" x 12" monthly envelopes. Write the item purchased on the receipt and on the front of the envelope. If the item needs to be returned to the store, the sales receipt can be located easily. At the end of the year, keep receipts for major purchases, such as appliances, jewelry, or suede coat, and discard the remainder.

3. *Current year's tax records*

Tax deductible receipts can be filed in the **PERSONAL BUSINESS FILE** in a file folder, in a large envelope furnished by your tax consultant, or in commercially designed tax files. The Simplex Tax Record File, a product of the National Blank Book Company, Inc. (Holyoke, MA 01040), is a compact booklet in which to store current tax papers. Each pocket page relates to a specific type of tax deduction, for instance, medical and dental or contributions. Space is provided on which to record income, expenses, and income summary. At the end of the year, remove papers for your tax consultant. Earnings statements can be discarded after they have been checked against the W-2 form.

The burden of proof concerning deductions is that of the taxpayer, not of the IRS. If records are poorly organized and inadequate, some deductions might be disallowed and a penalty incurred. Having to piece together a year's worth of records at midnight on April 15th can be avoided by organizing records on a regular monthly basis.

4. *Loan payments due others*

Loan payment booklets can be filed behind the appropriate dates in the Action Notebook. If kept in this notebook, there is less chance that a payment will be missed. If payments are automatically paid from your checking account, be sure to make note of this in your financial records.

5. *Financial records*

I once read a sign that said, "Things always look greener in the other fellow's wallet." Perhaps it is easy to think that people who are financially secure have well organized records. This isn't always the case. Many people wish they could get their financial records in order, but stumble from one system to another looking for the perfect budget book to make everything balance. One basic manual for establishing control of the home budget and personal finances is *Bonnie's Household Budget Book* by Bonnie Runyan McCullough (NY: St. Martin's Press, 1983). It provides an eight-step plan for setting up a budget, monthly expense forms, and other useful charges, plus lots of sound advice.

Whatever format you use to record the income and outflow of your money, consider these two questions: 1) Do you consistently use your financial records? Many readers finish only the first chapter of books they buy or borrow. Similarly, many home managers resolve each January to keep track of every penny spent, but seldom succeed beyond February 15. 2) Where do you keep your financial records? Where the records are kept may have some bearing on consistency of use, although self-discipline is really the key. Keep financial records that involve daily income and expenses in an accessible location. The closer they are kept to the Action Notebook, the better. A cubbyhole in a desk, a letter tray, or the first drawer of a desk would be within easy reach.

Nonpending Personal Business Papers

The second type of papers in a **PERSONAL BUSINESS FILE** are nonpending and are considered semi-active. Such papers include certificates, contracts, and receipts that need to be retained for a longer term for documentation purposes. If you use a location outside your home to store originals, make copies to keep in a **PERSONAL BUSINESS FILE** at home. According to the United States Department of Agriculture brochure, *Keeping Family/Household Records; What to Discard,* "A guideline as to what goes in and what stays out of your safe deposit box might be: put it in if you can't replace it or if it would be costly or troublesome to replace."

Use the PREFIX METHOD to establish a **PERSONAL BUSINESS FILE** with the prefix letters, PB, for the code. This is how a sample **PERSONAL BUSINESS FILE INDEX** might appear:

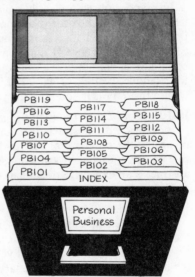

PB101 - *Certificates*
PB102 - *Insurance Policies*
PB103 - *Real Estate (or Rental)*
PB104 - *Home Improvement*
PB105 - *Vehicle Title*
PB106 - *Vehicle Repairs*
PB107 - *Education Records*
PB108 - *Household Inventory*
PB109 - *Health Records*
PB110 - *Pets' Records*
PB111 - *Investments*
PB112 - *Divorce Papers*
PB113 - *Funeral/Estate Plans*
PB114 - *Wallet Contents*
PB115 - *Adoption Papers*
PB116 - *Social Security*
PB117 - *Employment History*
PB118 - *Income History*
PB119 - *Retirement*

If you were taking the one-minute quiz at the beginning of the chapter and you had a **PERSONAL BUSINESS FILE INDEX,** you could immediately answer the questions this way:

1.   Q. You are selling your home. You made substantial improvements in your home. Can you prove it?
     A. Of course. I'll get folder PB104 for you.

2.   Q. You have just lost your wallet. The $100 wasn't so important, but the papers in it were. What papers were in it?

148 • File... Don't Pile!

A. Just a second. PB114 will provide that information.

3.   Q. You are registering your child for school. Can you verify her birthdate and immunizations?
A. Yes, in folders PB101 and PB109.

Let's briefly examine the entries in this Paperdex.

PB101 - *Certificates*

Include birth, marriage, and death records of immediate family members. Copies of certificates for extended family members should be filed with genealogy or family history papers.

The original documents should be kept in a safe place such as a safe deposit box. Keep copies only in a **PERSONAL BUSINESS FILE** at home. Many times an original is not necessary for documentation and the home copy can be used.

PB102 - *Insurance*

Insurance policies are easily replaced by insurance companies. If you use a safe deposit box for your important papers, file a list of insurance policy numbers in it. Keep original insurance policies in the **PERSONAL BUSINESS FILE** at home. If you have a number of policies, one folder might not provide adequate space to file them. Divide them, for example, PB102$_a$ - Health & Life Insurance, and PB102$_b$ - Car and House Insurance. If you rent, file your Tenants Homeowners Policy.

PB103 - *Real Estate (or Rental Agreement)*

Include deeds, abstracts, property taxes, appraisals, and any data regarding the purchase of the residence, including related fees such as title search. Original documents should be kept in a safe place. An abstract is an expensive document to replace. If you rent an apartment or home, this folder could include the lease agreement.

PB104 - *Home Improvement*

If you have made major home improvements — such as remodeling the kitchen, family room addition, waterproofing the basement — keep receipts for the improvements. If you sell your home, documentation of the improvements may be necessary.

PB105 - *Vehicle Title*

Vehicle titles, if this applies in your state, are necessary documents in transferring ownership. While titles can be replaced if lost, it may take weeks and can be costly. A family who had just moved into a new home decided to sell one of their cars. They searched through packing boxes for two weeks trying to locate the car title. By the end of the second week, the small missing document was a source of irritation.

Should a small piece of paper be able to exercise such control? The question applies whether it is a missing car title, a check, or football tickets. Keep vehicle titles in a safe place. A photocopy can be kept at home if you use a safe deposit box. After an accident I had, it saved time for my insurance agent because I had quick access to information concerning my car.

PB106 - *Vehicle Repairs*
The length of time to keep receipts for repair work on vehicles is a personal decision. Some people retain records for the life of the car, others for only one year. If a part on a car is replaced at 15,000 miles, it is newer than the rest of the vehicle and may affect the resale value. If you've repaired a specific part on your car and the manufacturer later recalls it, you can get a rebate if you can prove the work was done. In either case, a receipt would be helpful to have. If you have several vehicles, you can use more than one folder, for instance, $PB106_a$ - Station Wagon; $PB106_b$ - Van.

PB107 - *Education Records*
Include copies of grade transcripts, GRE scores, and so forth. While the copies do not serve as legal proof of course work or degrees, they are useful for your information. Valid documents must be sent directly from registrar's offices to whomever needs the verification.

PB108 - *Household Inventory*
You can create your own booklet in which to itemize your household inventory or obtain one free from your insurance agent. Stationery stores sell inexpensive booklets. An excellent one is *Dome Inventory of Household and Personal Property* by Nicholas Picchione (Dome Publishing Company, Inc., Providence, RI 02903). Meeting the time deadline by which to complete a claim form is eased tremendously by having a written inventory. An itemized list alone does not document the value or ownership of lost goods, however. *A household inventory should include the following:*

1. *Validation of purchase costs and ownership*
   Include sales receipts, bills, vouchers, canceled checks, and professional appraisals. Provide description and serial numbers whenever possible. Don't forget to add sales tax in the cost. Newlyweds would be wise to begin immediately to establish a household inventory complete with receipts.

2. *Photographs*
   Take color photos, slides, movie footage, or videotapes of your household items. Include detailed close-up views, such as the bottom of each piece of one setting of your fine china. Also photograph a long-range view, i.e., your 91-piece service-for-twelve china arranged on a table draped with a dark cloth; have someone in the family stand in the picture. Photograph two or three views of entire rooms. If you have a large collection of books, plates, or records, take

pictures of each wall or shelf. Don't just open a closet door and take a picture. Be as specific and thorough as you can. It will pay off. One family recovering from a fire didn't have any photos. Family members had to pore through relatives' albums to find photos of their living room in order to piece together an inventory.

3. *Verbal description*
Tour each room of your home with microphone in hand and tape record the contents. Spend as much time as you can in each room describing each item you see in the room.

Many police departments have an Operation Identification program. An identification number is assigned and recorded in the police office. The police department lends engraving tools at no charge so the identification number can be marked on belongings.

There are businesses that offer the service of complete home inventories. Some use Polaroid cameras, others use videotape to do a photo inventory. Be sure to investigate the reputation of the business beforehand and whether or not it is bonded. Ask for referrals.

Do NOT keep your household inventory in your home unless it is kept in a fire resistant safe. Put the inventory in the safe deposit box or give it to a close relative. A second copy can be kept at home, in which to note new items purchased and items that have been discarded or sold at a garage sale. Once a year, use the second copy to update the original.

Check with your insurance company concerning a replacement rider and how it would affect replacing items in your inventory. Regular insurance policies deduct a depreciation, but many companies also provide special replacement riders. Items damaged or stolen, covered by such riders, are replaced at today's market price. The cost of the rider depends on the value of the items being insured. The requirement of this rider, naturally, is that the item protected by it must be replaced. You cannot simply collect the money.

PB109 - *Health Records*
File a list of health records for each family member. Include information that applies:

Blood Type	Blood Pressure
Blood Donations	Cholesterol
Allergies (Reactions and Prescriptions)	Pap Smear
Immunizations	Breast Exam
Contagious Diseases	Pelvic Exam
Serious Illnesses or Injury	Eye Exam (including eyeglasses
Surgery (When, where, physician,	or contact lens prescriptions)
for what, and complications)	Dental Records
Physical Examinations	Medicare and Medicaid
Chest X-ray	

This information can be divided into separate folders depending on how much material needs to be filed.

PB110 - *Pets' Records*

Registration records, vaccinations, veterinarian's bills, record of offspring, and other information about your pets should be filed. Photos can be included for use in case a pet strays.

PB111 - *Investments*

Investment papers such as government bonds, certificates for securities, stocks, and municipal and industrial bonds are important documents and should be kept in a safe place. Venita Van Caspel's *Money Dynamics for the 1980s* indicates that professionals take care of the recordkeeping of mutual funds. Ms. Van Caspel says, " . . . keep the last confirmation you receive that year, and you will have a complete record of your account. The mutual fund also will send you (and IRS) a form 1099, showing the dividends and capital gains paid to you for the year. This you will want to keep and attach to your federal income tax return."

Your financial records should include a list of the companies in which you have invested, the type, certificate numbers, dates purchased, number of shares, bonds' face value, purchase price, and buying expense. Indicate ownership, date of sale, number of units sold, selling price, selling expense, and amount of profit or loss. There are booklets available that make this recordkeeping easier.

PB112 - *Divorce Papers*

File a certified copy of the judgment and decree in a marital dissolution and any correspondence with attorneys necessary for your records. In addition, if you retain the house or car or other property used as collateral, you must send a certified copy of your divorce decree to the title holder by certified mail.

PB113 - *Funeral/Estate Plans*

Inexpensive booklets can be purchased to record information concerning your personal estate. Organizing vital information will spare others fear, frustration, and foolish spending that often results from lack of knowledge. Include a general list of your personal and financial counselors with addresses and telephone numbers. Include the following as they apply:

Accountant	Doctor
Attorney	Employer
Auto insurance agent	Executor(s) of estate
Banker	Executor of will
Business partner	Eye doctor
Dentist	Financial advisor

Funeral director
Homeowner's insurance agent
Life insurance agent
Medical insurance agent
Power of attorney
Religious advisor

Social Security office
Stockbroker
Tax consultant
Trustee of estate
Union representative
Other

Include information regarding your insurance, assets and liabilities, survivor benefits, income tax, bank account numbers, and location of documents. File a copy of the will, codicils, location of the original will and children's guardian's names. Include your cemetery deed and burial information. The deceased *can* have a say in the plans, even the songs, if funeral instructions are provided beforehand. List names of people or organizations to be notified and plans for donation of body parts for transplantation or of entire body to medical or dental school. Record any information you would naturally want others to know in the event of your death. You are never too young to compile this information. Do NOT file funeral and personal estate papers in a safe deposit box. It may be a time before survivors are permitted to open the sealed box.

PB114 - *Wallet Contents*

If your wallet is lost or stolen, more than just credit cards need to be replaced. Instead of making a list of the contents, place the cards and papers face down on a photocopy machine and copy them. For a minimal cost you can have an 8½" x 14" piece of paper showing pictures of your wallet contents. Credit cards can be registered as part of the membership for many automobile clubs. Some organizations and businesses charge a small fee for the same service. If you are missing your cards, you only need to make one phone call to report the loss. When traveling or shopping, take only those credit cards you will be using. Keep an inventory of the contents of your suitcase as well. An itemized list is necessary to claim insurance in the event it is lost.

PB115 - *Adoption Papers*

File a copy of adoption decrees and any correspondence with attorneys and the adoptive agency necessary for your records.

PB116 - *Social Security*

Keep a record of Social Security numbers for anyone in your household. Even if your children are grown and have left home, there may be occasions when this information is needed and you'll have it. If you lose your card, contact a Social Security office to obtain a duplication. If you change your name, you can get a new card from the Social Security office.

PB117 - *Employment History*

Instead of creating a new resume each time you change positions, keep your old ones and simply update them. Record dates to and from employed, employer, address, position held, and responsibilities. Other information to include on your resume is education, professional membership, activities in college, current activities and interests, and references.

PB118 - *Income History*

A record of one's income including salary and commissions, bank interest, returns on stocks and bonds, and loan payments received from others would provide an overview, especially if kept over a period of years, and would aid in setting goals. Include a net worth statement with your income history records. A form can be used to list your assets, obligations, and the difference between them. A graph chart would be the most visual overall net worth statement.

PB119 - *Retirement*

Include papers regarding employment and/or self-employment benefits, pension or annuity, Individual Retirement Account or Keogh Plan, and profit sharing.

Other Important Documents

Other important papers to keep in a safe place include: citizenship or naturalization; copyrights and patents; passports; paid-up notes, liens, contracts that either you owe or are owed you, both outstanding and paid up; military discharge papers, teaching contracts and certificates, and any documents that are either government or court recorded.

The following personal business papers can be filed behind the PB119 folder.

Warranties and Guarantees

Years ago, in an effort to centralize my warranties and guarantees, I used the traditional Crammed Shoe Box method. This was ineffective because I could never find what I wanted when I needed it. My second attempt was the Bulging Binder approach. You can purchase an inexpensive and compact answer to the problem — the Warranty and Manual Organizer, available from Current, Inc., Colorado Springs, CO 80918-3150. Or you can create your own booklet with pocket pages for categories of products normally receiving a warranty or maintenance manual. Include such categories as Large Kitchen Appliances, Small Kitchen Appliances, and Home Furnishing Appliances.

Bank Statements and Canceled Checks

The main purpose of a bank statement is to provide a means for balancing your checkbook. If you find a discrepancy, use the statement and your canceled checks to substantiate your position. Opinions conflict on how long bank statements should be retained. Although there are exceptions, bank statements used as documentation for tax purposes should be saved for the IRS three-year statute of limitations. It isn't necessary to keep all canceled checks. No one is going to audit you on checks written for $2.10 at the corner grocery or for $5 at a Tupperware party. Retain checks for major purchases and for anything related to your home. Any records or canceled checks associated with currently owned assets must be retained until three years after those assets are sold. Consequently, it may be necessary to keep some checks, such as those for your residence, land, expensive jewelry, and camera equipment, for your entire lifetime. If you do not have a sales receipt for an item, sometimes a canceled check is your only recourse. Canceled checks used for documentation for tax purposes should be retained until the statute of limitations expires for an IRS audit.

Checks can be stored in the boxes in which they came or filed numerically in a small shoe box. The box can be kept in the back of the drawer in which you keep the **PERSONAL BUSINESS FILE.**

Past Years' Tax Records

How long do you need to retain income tax returns from previous years? The answer varies. Normally, the IRS has three years from the filing deadline for conducting audits on Federal income tax returns. If you omitted 25% of your gross income, however, the statute of limitations is extended to six years. If you failed to file a return or if you filed a proved fraudulent return, the statute extends indefinitely. Time limitations vary across the country, so check your state's laws.

Taxpayers have three years in which to claim a refund. Once the statute has expired, a refund can be collected, but a percentage is withheld.

Due to the normal three-year limitation, many accountants advise their clients to retain tax returns for three years. If you are planning to income average, retain your records for the prior four-year period. To be on the safe side, tax returns should be held for six years.

If you own a small business, keep books and records available at all times. Recordkeeping requirements are outlined in the pamphlet, *Recordkeeping for a Small Business* available from the Superintendent of Documents, U.S. Government Printing Office, Washington, DC 20402.

A Little at a Time

If establishing a **PERSONAL BUSINESS FILE** causes you to feel like filing yourself in PB113 and calling it quits, it's understandable. The task is a big one. But the benefits are even greater. Take consolation in the fact that setting up a **PERSONAL BUSINESS FILE** doesn't have to be done in one day. Once the **PERSONAL BUSINESS** papers are centralized, break the job of organizing them into manageable assignments. For example:

1st. *Organize pending papers.* You deal with these most frequently.

2nd. *Organize nonpending papers* (excluding household inventory and funeral/estate plans) into two piles and follow directions for each:

Pile 1. Papers to be filed in a "maximum" security location, such as a safe.
a. If the maximum security location is outside the home, photocopy the papers and put the original records in this safe place. File photocopies of originals with other "minimum" security papers.
b. If the maximum security location is inside the home, establish a **PERSONAL BUSINESS FILE**. File the folders in your safe.

Pile 2. Papers to be filed in a "minimum" security location, such as a metal filing cabinet.
a. Establish a **PERSONAL BUSINESS FILE**.
b. File the folders in a file drawer.

3rd. *Organize papers concerning household inventory and funeral/ estate plans.*

Organizing a household inventory and funeral/estate plans are such overwhelming jobs to most people. It isn't until a fire or flood or death occurs that many people feel motivated to action. Usually prior to a cruise or cross-country trip people feel prompted to complete their estate plans.

A fire is traumatic enough without having to grope through ashes to trigger your memory of your household items. Plan now to inventory your items and note who you want to leave certain items to, even if you change your mind later. Take the time to discuss your personal estate with at least one individual. You'll both have peace of mind.
a. Set a target date for completing your household inventory.
b. Set a target date for completing your funeral/estate plans.

Every individual has *some* personal business papers, even if it's only a birth certificate with wet ink.

Summary

What is a PERSONAL BUSINESS FILE?

The purpose of a PERSONAL BUSINESS FILE is to document.

Where should a PERSONAL BUSINESS FILE be stored?

Originals
1. Home Safe
2. Safe Deposit Box
3. Vault

Copies
1. File cabinet
2. Desk drawer
3. Tote Box

How long are Personal Business Papers stored?

This depends on individual records.

Key Pending Personal Business Papers

1. Monthly, unpaid bills, new and ongoing
2. Unpaid sales receipts
3. Current year's tax records
4. Loan payments due others
5. Financial records

Key Nonpending Personal Business Papers

1. Certificates
2. Insurance Policies
3. Real Estate (or Rental Agreement)
4. Home Improvement
5. Vehicle Title
6. Vehicle Repairs
7. Education Records
8. Household Inventory
9. Health Records
10. Pet Records
11. Investments
12. Divorce Papers
13. Funeral/Estate Plans
14. Wallet Contents
15. Adoption Papers
16. Social Security
17. Employment History
18. Income History
19. Retirement

Other Nonpending Personal Business Papers

Warranties and guarantees, bank statements and canceled checks, past tax records, citizenship or naturalization, copyrights and patents, passports, paid up notes, liens, contracts either you owe or are owed you (both outstanding and paid up), military discharge papers, professional contracts and certificates, and any documents that are either government or court recorded. Keys, inventory of safe deposit box, and photo negatives.

Chapter Ten
From Chaos to Control

I'll File That Pile ... Tomorrow

Some people cope with the disorder in their homes and seek ways to gain control over the clutter. Others merely want better access to their papers without requiring that every book, magazine, or paper has an exact place. As one client said to me, "I prefer living in comfortable chaos. I'd feel like I had died if *everything* were put away."

How would you feel if you had established your files, had no more "Bags of Life" in your closets and had cleared the kitchen counters? People react differently to orderliness. Some people say, "Good. Now that this house is in order, I want it to stay this way." Other people might respond like this to that statement: "Not if I'm around, it won't." One client told me that an orderly house to her means that people will be coming. She said, "If people aren't coming over, an orderly house seems lonely. I don't feel lonely, even if I'm alone, in a messy house."

I have frequently asked the question, "After you've done such a splendid job in getting organized, do you want to look like the cover of this book again?" Some answer, "No, I don't want to backslide. Show me how I can keep up now that I'm caught up." Others reply, "I know from past experience I will get sidetracked and things will get messy again. But if I call it backsliding, I'll feel like I've failed. I consider it more as spiraling because each time that I work at getting organized, I am better off than I was before. I can see some progress. It would be helpful to have some system for keeping up, though."

Few people come home from a class or meeting with papers in hand, dutifully "skate" right to their files, and put their papers away. They usually say, "I'm tired. The family is hungry. I'll just pile this stuff here. Tomorrow I'll put those papers in my marvelous files." Piles of papers

159

grow on top of the microwave, the piano, and the little table in the front foyer. One woman said to me, "I think paper breeds in those places. I clean off the counters, and before you know it, they're piled high again. The chaos sneaks up on me." Most homes have certain low spots that are notorious dropping off points for incoming papers. This chapter describes a Four-Step Maintenance Plan that teaches you how to keep up with your filing without having to file every day.

The Four-Step Maintenance Plan

Step 1. Establish Interim Files

The first step in the Four-Step Maintenance Plan is *to establish interim places in which to store to-be-filed papers.*

In many homes papers settle spontaneously wherever letters are opened, school bags are dropped, or pockets are emptied. By designating a temporary storage place for to-be-filed papers, you will have a spot to put those papers that otherwise might stack up on the kitchen counter.

There are two kinds of interim files: 1) the vertical sorter and 2) the prefiling box or folder.

The *vertical sorter* is a series of plastic filing pockets that mount on the wall. Assign a pocket to each family member or to a specific category of papers. Additional pockets can be snapped on when needed. Incoming papers can be stored temporarily in the vertical sorter until you have time to distribute them to their designated permanent files or to the prefiling boxes or folders described later.

Since the purpose of the vertical sorter is to provide an orderly substitute for the notorious low spots, install it in an accessible location. It is difficult enough to conquer the habit of piling papers. Don't create a second and unrealistic expectation of putting papers in an interim file that is kept in an out-of-the-way location. This may mean the vertical sorter should be kept in the kitchen, because in many homes this area often serves as the hub.

I had a client whose daily influx of papers always piled up on the kitchen counters and the dining room table. She had a desk in the bedroom for personal papers and an office in her basement for paperwork involving her position as president of a major nonprofit organization. But because her home was large and her schedule was busy, she didn't immediately go to those areas to file her papers. The vertical sorter provided an interim storage place to maintain the to-be-filed papers so they didn't pile up. On her way to her personal desk or to her basement office, she removed the papers from the vertical sorter and took them with her. If she still didn't have time to actually file the papers, she transferred them to another "holding tank," the prefiling box.

The *prefiling box* is a small box about the size of one in which 100 file folders are packed. One box is used for each category that gen- erates many nonpending papers. Mark the category, followed by the words, ... TO BE FILED, on the 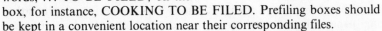 box, for instance, COOKING TO BE FILED. Prefiling boxes should be kept in a convenient location near their corresponding files.

The *prefiling folder* is used if a category accumulates only a few papers. Mark the category, followed by the words, ... TO BE FILED, on the folder, for instance, COOKING TO BE FILED. Prefiling folders should be kept directly behind the Paperdex in their corresponding files.

Some people I've worked with have reported that it's helpful to schedule one morning every month to file papers they've accumulated. Each person must discover what works best for him or her. One good maintenance yardstick is to file when the prefiling boxes or folders are full. I received a telephone call from Jo Brown, a student in one of my workshops who felt discouraged, however, because six months had lapsed since she had last filed. "My filing is just like all the other unfinished projects in my house," she said. "When I took the workshop, I was all excited. I filed like crazy for about two weeks. Now I'm all behind, and it's so depressing."

I asked Jo where she kept the papers she had accumulated. She said she remembered the centralizing step and this helped her to keep similar papers boxed together. However, after six months of not filing, the backlog of unfiled recipes seemed overwhelming to her. Even though Jo didn't realize it, she had followed the first step in the Four-Step Maintenance Plan by creating a place in which to store her to-be-filed papers.

If you maintain prefiling boxes or folders for each category, two things will happen. First, you can stop worrying about having to file every week. Second, you can breathe easier when you wish to find a particular paper during the interim period. The paper you want will be either in its file, or it will be in one of the interim files.

Bonnie McCullough, author of *Totally Organized,* says, "To be in control, you don't have to be caught up."

Step 2. Establish Paper Centers

The second step in the Four-Step Maintenance Plan is *to establish major paper centers in which to store paperwork.* The centers include papers kept in established files as well as papers in prefiling boxes or folders to be filed.

Many people have difficulty applying the old saying, "A place for everything, and everything in its place." This is especially true concerning papers. I prefer to word the adage this way: "A *vicinity* for everything, and everything in its *vicinity.*" Each vicinity or *center* stores certain kinds of papers. For example:

CENTER	KINDS OF PAPERS STORED
Personal Business Center	**PERSONAL BUSINESS FILE** (see Chapter 9); **MONEY MANAGEMENT FILE** (see Chapter 5)
Personal Correspondence Center	**PERSONAL CORRESPONDENCE FILE; GREETING CARD FILE** (see Chapter 8)
Food Management Center	**COOKING FILE** (see Chapter 4); Grocery Store Lists (see Chapter 8)
Household Management Center	Action Notebook; Rolodex (see Chapter 8)
Personal Interest Center	Each family member's personal papers: class notes, hobbies, and interests
Special Project Center	PTA President; School Closing Committee
Professional Business Center	In-home business-related papers

If papers are kept in designated centers, you stand a better chance of finding a specific paper when you want it, instead of two weeks later. Without centers, you have unlimited options of where to begin looking for that special item.

Paper doesn't confine itself to one room, nor is it used in one area of the home. Locating the centers has to be based both on where it may be ideal to have them, as well as on where you can fit them. Look first in the places where people do things. Look first in the kitchen for a place to locate the Food Management Center. Look first in the dining room for a space to set up a Personal Correspondence Center if this is where you write letters (see Chapter Eight, section on Personal Correspondence Center). It may not always be possible to set up a center in the area you do things, but look in those areas first — as opposed to going around the house and simply grabbing any unused space to create centers.

Draw a sketch of your floor plan, and note the centers in each room. This helps you to visualize the locations, specifically, the vicinities where incoming papers should be drawn magnetically.

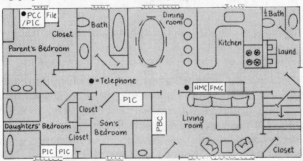

Organizing a center may be as simple as cleaning out a drawer for letter-writing supplies or a matter of finding some place for a small filing cabinet. *A center does not have to be a full-scale desk.* One woman relates that an old Hoosier cabinet in the pantry served as a "desk" while she was involved on a PTA committee. She cleared off one shelf and used it for this particular project. When she finished the job, she used the shelf for something else. "I am chronically involved," she said. "If it isn't a petition drive for a stoplight on the corner, it's another special issue. Each activity seems to produce six months of paper, and I need special places for them."

The cabinet wasn't a desk in a formal sense, but it served effectively as one. A center might be a red suitcase or a plastic totebox. It may be a sawhorse-door combination desk or an oak rolltop desk. The main point is that a space is designated as the location where certain kinds of papers are stored.

Step 3. Use Code-a-Pile Method

The third step in the Four-Step Maintenance Plan is *to code a large pile of papers at one time before filing them into the folders.*

When Jo Brown called me about her backlog of recipes, she wanted a quick solution to help her get caught up on her filing. I gave her sixty seconds of instructions and told her to go to it. She called back the next morning very excited. She couldn't believe it. Jo had filed a six-month accumulation of recipes in one afternoon. She felt free again and could hardly wait to clean up the rest. The simple instructions I gave Jo are Steps 3 and 4 of the Four-Step Maintenance Plan.

Once a file is established, as Jo Brown did her **COOKING FILE,** it serves as a foundation of subject headings from which papers can be quickly coded. The Code-a-Pile step requires three items: the box of papers to be filed, the Paperdex for the specific category, and a pencil. File folders and markers are *not* needed for this step.

This step involves six actions:

1. Remove an item from the prefiling box or folder.
2. Determine the subject for the item.
3. Look up the subject in the Paperdex to learn the assigned code.
4. Print the code on the item in the upper right-hand corner.
5. Enter appropriate cross references in Paperdex.
6. Set aside item to be filed; repeat process on the next item.

If the subject is not listed in the Paperdex, decide whether to enter it as a new subject or whether the item should be interfiled with another already-established subject. If the subject is a new entry, do not make a file folder for it at this time. Simply print the newly assigned code on the item to be filed, and continue coding the rest of the papers in the pile. File folders for new entries will be made during Step 4.

Papers in a prefiling box or folder can be coded at various times and places. I take materials with me to the backyard or to the park and work there while the children are playing. I code papers while watching television. The prefiling box or folder and the Paperdex are so portable, it's easy to catch up on your filing anywhere. I even work on my files in the dentist's waiting room. It's more productive than rereading magazines I already have clipped at home.

The main advantage of the Code-a-Pile step is that it saves a tremendous amount of time and energy. Coding large piles of papers in one category is a quick process. Since only coding is accomplished during this step, not actual filing, it minimizes the motions spent per item. If there is some doubt in determining the subject of an item, set the paper aside and continue coding the rest of the pile. Don't lose momentum. A friend with a similar category may have suggestions about where the problem items can be filed.

When all the papers are coded, they are ready for the fourth step, to be speed-filed. If time doesn't permit filing the papers at this point, put the coded papers back in the prefiling box or folder. The fourth step can be done later.

Step 4. Use the Speed-filing Approach

The fourth step in the Four-Step Maintenance Plan is *to use the speed approach to file the coded papers.*

The speed-filing step requires the following items: the prefiling box or folder of coded papers to be filed, the established file (for example, the box or drawer in which the **COOKING FILE** is kept), a supply of file folders, and a wide-tip felt marking pen in the appropriate color for the category.

This step involves three actions:

1. Remove all the coded papers from the prefiling box or folder.
2. Sort the coded papers on the floor or on a table.
   If the category uses the A-Z METHOD: Sort the papers according to the letter in the code. Don't be concerned with the number in the code.

If the category uses the PREFIX METHOD: Sort the papers in numerical order according to the number in the code.

3. File the coded papers in the folders one letter or number at a time, for instance, all the A's first; B's next.

If there is no folder in the file drawer for a code, it means this was a newly entered subject in the Paperdex during the Code-a-Pile step. Make a folder at this time using the appropriate colored wide-tip felt marking pen. Be sure to check which file folder — left, center, or right tab — is needed before marking the folder.

A large accumulation of papers can be filed very quickly if it has been coded. It doesn't matter what length of time has lapsed between Steps 3 and 4. Also, two different people can do the two steps. One family I've worked with has five daughters. The mother codes a pile of papers, and the daughters file them.

Perhaps you'll have a six-month interruption in filing, as Jo Brown did. Or maybe it will only be three months. It doesn't matter. Don't let interruptions allow you to think getting your papers organized is an impossible task. Interrupted? Of course you'll be interrupted. Count on it. Just remember:

> It is not how fast you get it filed — but
> how fast you can find it that counts.

Dartnell Professional Secretary's Handbook
Dartnell Corp., Chicago

Summary
Four-Step Maintenance Plan

Step 1. *Establish Interim Files.*
    1. Vertical Sorter
    2. Prefiling Boxes
    3. Prefiling Folders

Step 2. *Establish Paper Centers.*
    1. Determine what centers are needed to store paperwork.
    2. Determine where centers should be located.
    3. Determine what equipment will be used as the center, for example, desk, drawer, totebox.

Step 3. *Use Code-a-Pile Method.*
    1. Remove item from prefiling box or folder.
    2. Determine subject for the item.
    3. Look up subject in Paperdex to learn assigned code.
    4. Print code on item.
    5. Enter appropriate cross references in Paperdex.
    6. Set item to be filed aside; repeat process on next item.

Step 4. *Use Speed-filing Approach.*
    1. Remove coded papers from prefiling box or folder.
    2. Sort coded papers according to letter or number.
    3. File coded papers in folders.

Epilog

Here I am, still clipping and filing. But I'm relaxed, because it is a wonderful feeling to be able to find my treasures when I want them. What motivated me to find a system was pure desperation. Some workshop participants have shared more subtle purposes for learning how to file the paper in their lives. Some are psychological reasons, such as, to free myself from the burden of wishing I were organized or to conquer my fear of filing. (Is the latter like Math Anxiety?) One woman confessed she was attending a File ... Don't Pile workshop because her psychiatrist had sent her! Some are physical reasons, such as, to reduce my high blood pressure or to find my house!

You have your own unique reasons — reasons that motivated you to buy this book or to check it out from the library.

Acting on the ideas in a book is another matter, however. Some people buy a how-to book and underline in it and show it to their friends. They say, "I just love this little book," but they never quite get around to doing what it teaches. What inspires people to action? If it weren't for the cross-country move several years ago that triggered me into getting organized, I'd probably *still* be piling magazines in my closets.

Some people move quickly toward the light at the end of the tunnel, while others struggle to get started. What causes this isn't necessarily a matter of belief in the subject matter. It isn't that cut and dried. I've believed in many diet plans in my life. Sometimes time, money, family cooperation, space, and even personalities affect how and when people are motivated to get organized.

An anonymous author wrote, "No age or time of life, no position or circumstance, has a monopoly on success. Any age is the right age to start doing!"

Bibliography

Organization

Aslett, Don. *Clutter's Last Stand*. Cincinnati, OH: Writer's Digest, 1984.

Better Homes and Gardens. *Kitchen Projects You Can Build*. Des Moines, IA: Meredith, 1977.

_____. *Storage Projects You Can Build*. Des Moines, IA: Meredith, 1977.

Brace, Pam and Peggy Jones. *Sidetracked Home Executives*. New York, NY: Warner Books, 1981.

Coulthart, Bev. *How to Organize Your Family's Photographs*. St. Paul: Heirloom Photo, 1986. (532 Bayview Ct., Shoreview, MN 55112)

Evatt, Crislynne. *How to Organize Your Closet . . . and Your Life!* New York: Ballantine, 1980.

Fulton, Alice and Pauline Hatch. *It's Here . . . Somewhere*. Cincinnati, OH: Writer's Digest, 1985.

Isaacs, Susan. *How to Organize Your Kid's Room*. New York: Ballantine, 1985.

Laury, Jean Ray. *The Creative Woman's Getting-It-All-Together at Home Handbook*. Fresno, CA: Hot Fudge Press, 1985. (4974 N. Fresno St., Ste. 444, Fresno, CA 93710)

McCullough, Bonnie. *401 Ways to Get Your Kids to Work at Home*. New York: St. Martin's Press, 1981.

_____ and Bev Cooper. *76 Ways to Get Organized for Christmas and Make it Special, Too*. New York: St. Martin's Press, 1982.

_____. *Totally Organized*. New York: St. Martin's Press, 1986.

Meadowbrook Reference Group. *The Household Handbook*. Deephaven, MN: Meadowbrook Press, 1981.

Pighetti, Toni. *The Nitty-Gritty Bare Bones Method of Housekeeping Calendar*. Oak Park, IL: TAM Assoc., Annual. (P.O. Box 285, Oak Park, IL 60303)

Reader's Digest. *Organize Yourself!* New York: Berkley Books, 1982.

Schofield, Deniece. *Confessions of a Happily Organized Family*. Cincinnati, OH: Writer's Digest, 1984.

_____. *Confessions of an Organized Housewife*. Cincinnati, OH: Writer's Digest, 1981.

Sunset Ideas for Children's Rooms and Play Yards. Menlo Park, CA: Lane Publishing Company, 1980.

Sunset Ideas for Garage, Attic and Basement Storage. Menlo Park, CA: Lane Publishing Company, 1982.

Ubell, Vivian and David Sumberg. *Check Lists: 88 Essential Lists to Help You Organize Your Life*. New York: Crown, 1982.

Winston, Stephanie. *Getting Organized: the Easy Way to Put Your Life in Order*. New York: Warner, 1978.

_____. *The Organized Executive*. New York: W.W. Norton, 1983.

Children's Stories on Organization

Bottner, Barbara. *Messy.* New York: Delacorte, 1979.
Calhoun, Mary. *The Pixy and the Lazy Housewife.* New York: Wm. Morrow and Company, 1969.
Drescher, Joan. *The Marvelous Mess.* Boston: Houghton Mifflin, 1980.
Fox, Paula. *Maurice's Room.* New York: Macmillan, 1966.
Krasilovsky, Phyllis. *The Man Who Wouldn't Do the Dishes.* Garden City, NY: Doubleday, 1950.
Kraus, Robert. *Another Mouse to Feed.* New York: Windmill, 1980.
Orgel, Doris. *Sarah's Room.* New York: Harper and Row, 1963.
Rockwell, Anne. *The Awful Mess.* New York: Four Winds Press, 1973.
Sharmat, Marjorie Weinman. *Mooch the Messy.* New York: Harper and Row, 1976.
_____. *Mooch the Messy Meets Prudence the Neat.* New York: Coward, 1979.
Tompert, Ann. *It May Come in Handy Someday.* New York: McGraw-Hill, 1975.
Wells, Rosemary. *Stanley and Rhoda.* New York: Dial, 1978.
Zemach, Margot. *To Hilda for Helping.* New York: Farrar, Straus and Giroux, 1977.
Zolotow, Charlotte. *May I Visit?* New York: Harper and Row, 1976.

Wardrobe Organization

Audette, Vicki. *Dress Better for Less.* Deephaven, MN: Meadowbrook, 1981.
Jackson, Carole. *Color Me Beautiful.* New York: Ballantine, 1980.
Kentner, Bernice. *Color Me a Season.* Concord, CA: Kenkra Publications, 1978.

Time Management

Baer, Jean. *Don't Say Yes When You Want to Say No.* New York: McKay, 1975.
Bliss, Edwin. *Getting Things Done.* New York: Bantam, 1976.
Davidson, Jim. *Effective Time Management.* New York: Human Science Press, 1978.
Ellis, Albert. *Overcoming Procrastination.* New York: Signet, 1978.
Fanning, Tony and Robbie Fanning. *Getting it All Done and Still Be Human.* New York: Ballantine, 1979.
Goldfein, Donna. *Everywoman's Guide to Time Management.* Millbrae, CA: Les Femmes Publications, 1977.
King, Pat. *How to Have All the Time You Need Every Day.* Wheaton, IL: Tyndale House Pub., Inc., 1975.
Knaus, William J. *Do It Now: How to Stop Procrastinating.* Englewood Cliffs, NJ: Prentice-Hall, 1979.
Lakein, Alan. *How to Get Control of Your Time and Your Life.* New York: McKay, 1973.

170 • File . . . Don't Pile!

MacKenzie, R. Alec. *The Time Trap: How to Get More Done in Less Time.* New York: AMACOM, 1972.
_____ and Kay Cronkite Waldo. *About Time! A Woman's Guide to Time Management.* New York: McGraw Hill, 1980.
Miller, Ruth W. *The Time Minder.* Chappaqua, NY: Christian Herald Books, 1980.
Moskowitz, Robert. *How to Organize Your Work and Your Life.* Garden City, NY: Dolphin, 1981.
Scott, Dru. *How to Put More Time in Your Life.* New York: Rawson, Wade, 1980.
Silcox, Diana. *Woman Time: Personal Time Management for Women Only.* New York: Wyden, 1980.
Smith, Manual J. *When I Say No, I Feel Guilty.* New York: Dial, 1977.
Wilt, Joy. *A Kid's Guide to Managing Time.* Waco, TX: Educational Products Division, Word, Inc., 1979.

Money Management

Hallman, G. Victor and Jerry S. Rosenbloom. *Personal Financial Planning.* 2nd ed. New York: McGraw-Hill, 1978.
Hill, Napoleon. *Think and Grow Rich.* Greenwich, CT: Fawcett, 1974.
McCullough, Bonnie Runyan. *Bonnie's Household Budget Book.* New York: St. Martin's Press, 1981.
Porter, Sylvia. *Sylvia Porter's New Money Book for the 80s.* New York: Avon, 1980.
Skousen, Mark. *High Finance on a Low Budget.* New York: Bantam, 1981.
Van Caspel, Venita. *Money Dynamics for the 1980s.* Reston, VA: Reston Publishing Co., 1980.

Psychology

de Castillejo, Irene Claremont. *Knowing Woman.* New York: Harper and Row, 1973.
Keirsey, David W. and Marilyn Bates. *Please Understand Me.* Del Mar, CA: Promethean, 1978.
Lawrence, Gordon. *People Types and Tiger Stripes.* 2nd edition. Gainesville, FL: Center for Applications of Psychological Type, Inc., 1982.
Meyers, Isabel Briggs and Peter Briggs Myers. *Gifts Differing.* Palo Alto, CA: Consulting Psychologists Press, Inc., 1980.
van der Post, Laurens. *Jung and the Story of Our Time.* New York: Pantheon, 1975.
Von Franz, Marie-Louise and James Hillman. *Lectures on Jung's Typology.* Irving, TX: Spring Publications, 1971.
Wheelwright, Joseph B. *Psychological Types.* San Francisco: C. B. Jung Institute of San Francisco, 1973.
Wickes, Frances G. *The Inner World of Childhood.* Rev. ed. Englewood Cliffs, NJ: Prentice-Hall, 1972.

Appendix

Directions for Use:

1. Terms that may be used as key subject headings are listed singly:
   Cakes
   Cheese
   Picnic Ideas

2. Terms narrow in scope that can be interfiled in larger key subject headings are cited in parentheses:
   Baked Alaska (Dessert or Ice Cream)
   Cream Puffs (Pastries)
   Popovers (Bread)

3. Key subject headings for which alternate terms may be used are cited following the word *or*. Additional suggestions follow a semicolon:
   Appreciation or Gratitude; Thanksgiving
   Evil or Wickedness
   Happiness or Joy

4. Key subject headings which may be subdivided are cited following a dash:
   Christmas — Cards
   Christmas — Decorations
   Christmas — Gifts

By using the subject headings in the Appendix you have a storehouse of terms to rely on. Another rich source of subject heading possibilities is the library. Check out books on the category of your interest, for example, gardening, and use the index in these books for ideas on how to word the terms. Two tips to follow in determining subject headings are:

1. *Be yourself* in wording the subject headings. Use the terms *you* commonly use when referring to them. If you think of several possibilities, select one under which to file the materials and cross reference the other terms.

2. *Be consistent* in entering information on the same topic under the same subject heading and not to file the materials under variant terms which might be used to express the same idea.

COOKING (Recipes, Foods, Nutrition, Diets)

A

Abalone (Shellfish)
Anchovies (Fish)
Appetizers or Hors d'
    Oeuvre; Tea Sandwiches;
    Canapes
Apples (Fruit)
Apricots (Fruit)
Artichokes (Vegetables)
Asparagus (Vegetables)

B

Bacon (Pork)
Bagels (Bread)
Baked Alaska (Dessert or
    Ice Cream)
Bananas (Fruit)
Barbecue
Bars
Batter Cooking
Beans
Beef
Berries (Fruit)
Beverages or Drinks
Biscuits (Bread)
Blender Cooking
Blintzes (Crepes or Batter
    Cooking)
Blueberries (Berries or
    Fruit)
Brains (Variety Meats)
Bread
Breakfasts
Brownies (Bars)
Broths (Soups)
Brunches
Buffets

C

Cabbage (Vegetables)
Cake Decorating
Cakes
Calorie Counting or
    Dieting; Weight Control

Camp Cooking or Outdoor
    Cooking
Canapes or Hors d'
    Oeuvre; Tea Sandwiches;
    Appetizers
Candy or Confections
Canned Foods
Canning
Cantaloupe (Melons or
    Fruit)
Casseroles or Hot Dishes
Cereals
Cheese
Cheesecakes (Pastries or
    Dessert)
Chicken (Poultry)
Chinese Cooking (Oriental
    Cooking)
Chocolate
Christmas Cooking
Clams (Shellfish)
Cobblers (Pies)
Coffee Cakes (Desserts)
Confections or Candy
Conserve or Jam
Consomme (Soups)
Cookies
Cooking — General
    Information
Cooking — Teaching
    Children
Cooking Tools or Kitchen
    Aids
Corned Beef (Beef)
Cornish Hens (Poultry)
Crabs (Shellfish)
Crayfish (Shellfish)
Cream Puffs (Pastries)
Crepes (Batter Cooking)
Crock Pot Cooking or
    Slow Pot Cooking
Croquettes (Batter
    Cooking)
Crullers (Doughnuts or
    Batter Cooking)
Curing (Salting or Food
    Storage)
Custards (Desserts)
Cut Up Cakes (Cakes or
    Cake Decorating)

D

Dairy Products
Dates (Fruit)
Deep Fat Frying (Frying)
Deer (Game)
Dehydrated Foods or
    Dried Foods
Desserts
Dietary Control
Dieting or Weight Control;
    Low Calorie Cooking
Dinners
Dips
Doughnuts (Batter
    Cooking)
Dressings — Salad
Dried Foods or
    Dehydrated Foods
Drinks or Beverages
Drying (Dehydrated Foods
    or Dried Foods)
Duckling (Poultry)
Dumplings (Bread)

E

Easter Cooking
Egg Cooking
Elk (Game)
Emergency Shelf Cooking
    (Fast Foods or Quick
    Cooking)

F

Fast Foods (Emergency
    Shelf Cooking or Quick
    Cooking)
Fish
Flan (Pastries)
Flavorings (Seasonings)
Fondue
Food Storage
Foreign Cooking or
    Gourmet
Frankfurters or Hot Dogs
Frappe (Frozen Desserts)
Freezing
Fritters (Batter Cooking)

F continued

Frostings or Icings
Frozen Desserts
Fruit
Fruit Leather (Dried
  Foods or Dehydrated
  Foods)
Frying

G

Game
Gardening
Garnishes
Gefilte Fish (Jewish
  Dishes)
Gelatins or Jello
Gingerbread Cooking
  (Christmas Cooking)
Glazes or Toppings
Gluten (Wheat)
Gnocchi (Italian Cooking)
Goose (Poultry)
Gourmet (Foreign
  Cooking)
Gravies (Sauces)
Ground Beef or
  Hamburger
Grouse (Game)

H

Ham (Pork)
Hamburger or Ground
  Beef
Hare (Game)
Health Food Cooking
Heart (Variety Meats)
Herbs and Spices or
  Seasonings
Holiday Cooking
Hominy (Corn)
Honey
Honey Ball Melon
  (Melons)
Honeydew Melon
  (Melons)
Hors d 'Oeuvre or
  Canapes; Tea
  Sandwiches; Appetizers
Hot Dishes or Casseroles
Hot Dogs or Frankfurters

I

Ice Cream
Ices (Frozen Dessert)
Icings or Frostings
Italian Cooking

J

Jams and Jellies
  (Preserves)
Japanese Cooking
  (Oriental Cooking)
Jello or Gelatins
Jelly Rolls (Desserts)
Jewish Dishes
Johnnycake (Bread)
Juices (Beverages or
  Drinks)

K

Kale (Cabbage or
  Vegetables)
Kidneys (Variety Meats)
Kitchen Aids or Cooking
  Tools
Kohlrabi (Cabbage or
  Vegetables)

L

Lamb (Meat)
Leeks (Onions)
Leftover Cooking
Legumes
Lemons and Limes (Fruit)
Lentils
Liver (Variety Meats)
Lobster (Shellfish)
Low Calorie Cooking or
  Dieting; Weight Control
Luncheons
Lunch Ideas

M

Macaroni (Noodles or
  Pasta)
Marinades (Sauces)
Marzipan (Candy)

Meal Planning
  (Menus/Menu Planning)
Measures and Weights
Meat
Meatloaf (Ground Beef or
  Hamburger)
Melons (Fruit)
Menus/Menu Planning
  (Meal Planning)
Microwave Cooking
Milk
Minerals (Nutrition)
Mini-Cookbooks
Mollusks (Shellfish)
Mousses (Desserts)
Mousses (Main Dish)
Mushrooms
Mussels (Shellfish)
Mutton (Meat)

N

Napoleon (Pastries)
Noodles (Pasta)
Nutrition
Nuts

O

Oat Cooking
Omelets (Egg Cooking)
One-Dish Meals
Onions
Opossum (Game)
Oranges (Fruit)
Oriental Cooking
Outdoor Cookery or Camp
  Cooking
Oysters (Shellfish)
Oxtail (Variety Meats)

P

Pancakes (Batter Cooking)
Parfaits (Frozen Desserts)
Partridge (Wildfowl or
  Poultry)
Pastries
Pates or Appetizer
Peaches (Fruit)
Pears (Fruit)
Peas (Vegetables)

P continued

Petits Fours (Cakes)
Pheasant (Wildfowl or
  Poultry)
Pickles
Pickling
Picnic Ideas
Pies
Pineapples (Fruit)
Pizza
Plums (Fruit)
Popovers (Bread)
Potatoes (Vegetables)
Poultry
Preserves (Jams and
  Jellies)
Pretzels (Bread)
Prunes (Fruit)
Puddings (Desserts)
Pumpkin (Vegetables)
Punch (Beverages or
  Drinks)

Q

Quail (Wildfowl or
  Poultry)
Quantity Cooking
Quiches (Egg Cooking)
Quick Cooking (Fast
  Foods or Emergency
  Shelf Cooking)

R

Rabbit (Game)
Raccoon (Game)
Raisins (Fruit)
Raspberries (Berries or
  Fruit)
Receptions
Relishes
Rhubarb
Rice
Rolls (Bread)
Root-cellaring (Food
  Storage)
Rosettes (Batter Cooking)

S

Salad Dressings
  (Dressings — Salad)
Salads — Fruit
Salads — Vegetable
Sandwiches
Sauces (Gravies)
Sausage
Scallops (Shellfish)
Scandinavian Cooking
Seasonings or Spices
Shellfish
Shrimp (Shellfish)
Slow Pot Cooking or
  Crock Pot Cooking
Smoking (Food Storage)
Smorgasbords
Snacks
Snails (Shellfish)
Souffles (Egg Cooking or
  Desserts)
Soups
Sourdough (Bread)
Soybeans
Spareribs (Pork)
Spices and Herbs or
  Seasonings
Sprouting
Squares (Bars)
Squirrel (Game)
Strawberries (Berries or
  Fruit)
Stuffing
Sugar
Summer Cooking
Sweetbreads (Variety
  Meats)
Syrups

T

Table Setting and Service
Tarts (Pastries)
Tea Sandwiches or
  Canapes; Hors d' Oeuvre;
  Appetizers

Terminology (Cooking —
  General Information)
Thanksgiving Cooking
Timbales (Egg Cooking)
Tomatoes
Tongue (Variety Meats)
Toppings (Glazes)
Torten (Cakes)
Trifle (Cakes)
Tripe (Variety Meats)
Turkey (Poultry)
Turnovers (Pastries)
Turtle (Shellfish)

V

Variety Meats
Veal (Beef)
Vegetables
Venison (Game)
Vitamins (Nutrition)

W

Waffles (Batter Cooking)
Watermelon (Melons)
Wedding Receptions
  (Receptions)
Weight Control or Dieting;
  Low Calorie Cooking
Weights and Measures
  (Cooking — General
  Information)
Wheat
Wildfowl (Poultry)

Y

Yams
Yeast
Yogurt

Z

Zucchini (Vegetables)
Zwieback (Bread)

CRAFTS

A

Accordion Folding (Paper
Folding)
Aluminum Foil or
Foilcraft
Antiquing
Applique

B

Baker's Clay (Dough
Sculpture)
Banners and Flags
Basketry
Batik and Tie Dye
Beadwork
Blacksmithing (Metalwork)
Block Printing
Body Painting or Skin
Painting
Bookbinding
Breadcraft

C

Calligraphy
Camp Craft
Candlemaking
Candlewicking
Caning
Cardboard
Cards or Greeting Cards
Cartooning
Centerpieces
Ceramics
China and Glass Painting
Christmas — Cards
Christmas — Decorations
Christmas — Gifts
Circus Ideas
Clothespin Craft
Collages
Colonial Craft
Color
Cork
Corncob Husks
Costumes
Crewel
Crochet

D

Decoupage
Dioramas
Dollhouses
Dolls
Dough Sculpture
Drawing
Dried Flowers
Driftwood
Dyeing

E

Easter
Egg Craft
Egg Decorating
Embossing (Leather Craft)
Embroidery
Enameling
Etching

F

Fabric Flowers
Fabric Printing
Father's Day Gifts
Fiberglass (Plastics)
Finger Painting
Flags (Banners and Flags)
Flowers — Dried or Dried
Flowers
Flowers — Fabric or
Fabric Flowers
Flowers — Paper or Paper
Flowers
Foilcraft
Folk Art
Framing or Picture
Framing

G

Games (Toys)
Gemcutting or Lapidary
Glass Etching
Glasswork
Gold Leafing
Greeting Cards or Cards
Growth Charts

H

Halloween
Hanukkah Crafts
Hardanger Lace
(Embroidery)

I

Ice Sculpture
Indian Crafts
Instruments or Musical
Instruments

J

Jewelry

K

Kilns
Kites
Knitting
Knotting or Macrame

L

Lacemaking
Lamps and Lampshades
Lapidary or Gemcutting
Leaf Prints
Leather
Linoleum (Block Printing)

M

Macaroni (Pastacraft)
Macrame or Knotting
Magic
Masks
May Baskets
Metalwork
Mobiles
Mosaics
Mother's Day Gifts
Murals
Musical Instruments or
Instruments

N

Nail Sculpture
Napkins and Napkin
  Folding
Nature Craft
Needlepoint

O

Oil Painting
Origami or Paper Folding

P

Paper Filigree (Papercraft)
Paper Flowers
Paper Folding or Origami
Paper Tole (Papercraft)
Papercraft
Papier Mache
Passover
Pastacraft
Patchwork
Photography
Picture Framing or
  Framing
Pinatas
Pioneer Craft
Plastics
Play Dough (Dough
  Sculpture)
Play Equipment
Pod and Cone Art
Posters
Pottery
Puppets
Puzzles (Toys)

Q

Quiet Books
Quilling (Papercraft)
Quilting

R

Raffia and Straw or
  Strawcraft
Recycling
Refrigerator Magnets
Resincraft
Ribboncraft
Rock Art
Rosemaling
Rosh Hashanah
Rugmaking

S

Sand Art
Sandcasting
Scissorscraft
Seedcraft
Serigraphy or Silk
  Screening
Shellcraft
Silhouettes
Silk Screening or
  Serigraphy
Sketching
Skin Painting or Body
  Painting
Soap Carving
Soap Making
Sockcraft
Soft Boxes
Spatter Painting
Spinning

Spoolcraft
Stained Glass
Stenciling
Strawcraft or Raffia and
  Straw
String Art
Sugar Cube Art
Swedish Huckwork

T

Tatting
Thanksgiving
Tie Dye or Batik and Tie
  Dye
Tincrafting
Tole (Papercraft)
Tooling (Leather Craft)
Tools and Equipment
Toothpick Art
Toys

V

Valentine's Day

W

Wallhangings
Watercolors
Weaving
Wheatweaving
Whittling (Woodworking)
Wire Art
Woodworking

Y

Yom Kippur

GARDENING

A

Air Layering
Animal Injury
Annuals
Arbor Day
Arboretum (Botanical
  Garden)

Arbors (Garden Fixtures)
Artificial Light Gardens
Autumn Gardens

B

Balcony Gardens (Porch
  Gardens)

Bamboo
Bank Gardens
Bedding Plants
Benches (Garden Fixtures)
Biennials
Bird Bath (Garden
  Fixtures)
Birdhouses (Garden
  Fixtures)

B continued

Bonsai
Borders or Edgings
Botanical Garden
  (Arboretum)
Bottle Garden
Breeding
Buds
Bulbs

C

Cactus or Succulents
Calendars or Garden
  Calendars
Catalogs
Children's Garden
Climate
Climbing Plants
Cold Frames
Color
Composts
Container Garden
Containers (Planters and
  Pots)
Courtyard Garden
Crabgrass (Lawns or
  Weeds)
Cultivation
Cut Flowers
Cuttings

D

Decorating with Plants
Desert Gardens
Dioecious Plants
Diseases — Plants
Diseases — Trees
Dish Gardens
Drainage (Watering)
Dried Flowers
Dwarfing

E

Edgings or Borders
Espaliering (Pruning)
Evergreens
Everlastings
Exotic Plants

F

Feeding Plants (Plant
  Food)
Fences (Garden Fixtures)
Ferns
Fertilizers (Plant Food)
Flower Arranging
Flower Garden
  (Flowerbeds)
Flowering Houseplants
Foliage
Fountains (Garden
  Fixtures)
Fruit
Fruit Trees
Furniture (Garden
  Fixtures)

G

Garden Calendars or
  Calendars
Garden Fixtures
Garden Maps
Garden Tables and Charts
Gates (Garden Fixtures)
Gift Plants
Grafting
Grass or Lawns
Green Manuring (Soul
  Improvement)
Greenhouses
Ground Covers

H

Hanging Gardens
Hardiness
Harvesting
Hedges
Herbs
Hotbeds
Houseplants

I

Indoor Plants
  (Houseplants)
Indoor Trees
Insect Pests (Pests)
Insecticides (Pest Control)
Irrigation (Watering)
Ivy

J

Japanese Gardens

K

Kitchen Gardens

L

Landscaping
Lawns or Grass
Lighting

M

Manure (Soil
  Improvement)
Maps (Garden Maps)
Mice (Animal Injury)
Miniature Gardens
Moles (Animal Injury)
Moving with Plants
  (Traveling with Plants)
Mulch
Mushrooms

N

Names of Plants
National Flowers
Night-Blooming Plants
Nitrogen (Fertilizers)
Nuts

O

Orchards
Orchids
Organic Gardens
Ornamental Plants
Ornamental Trees

P

Palms
Paths (Walks)
Patio and Terrace Gardens
Perennials
Pest Control
Pesticides (Pest Control)
Pests (Pest Control)

P continued

Plant Cases (Terrariums)
Plant Food
Planters and Pots
Play Areas
Poisonous Plants
Pools (Garden Fixtures)
Porch Gardens
Potting
Propagation
Pruning

Q

Quarantines

R

Rabbits (Animal Injury)
Rainfall
Raking
Rock Gardens
Rooftop Gardens
Roots
Roses

S

Sand Gardens
Seaside Gardens

Seedlings
Seeds
Shade
Shade Trees
Shrubs
Slopes (Bank Gardens)
Soil Improvement
Soils
Spring Gardens
Statues (Garden Fixtures)
Stems
Steps (Terraces)
Structures (Garden
  Fixtures)
Succulents or Cactus
Summer Gardens
Summerhouses (Garden
  Fixtures)

T

Talking to Plants
Temperature
Terrace Gardens (Patios
  and Terrace Gardens)
Terrariums
Toolhouse (Garden
  Fixtures)
Tools and Equipment
Topsoil (Soils)
Trailing Plants
Transplanting

Traveling with Plants
Trees (Fruit Trees; Indoor
  Trees; Ornamental Trees;
  Shade Trees)
Trellises (Garden Fixtures)
Tropical Plants
Tub Gardens
Tubers

V

Vases (Garden Fixtures)
Vegetable Gardens
Ventilation
Verandah Gardens (Porch
  Gardens)
Vines
Violets

W

Walks
Wall Gardens
Water Gardens
Watering
Weeds and Weeding
Window Boxes
Woodchucks (Animal
  Injury)
Workbench (Garden
  Fixtures)

HOME IMPROVEMENT

A

Additions, to house
  (Remodeling)
Adhesives
Air Conditioning or
  Cooling System
Air Control
Alarm Systems
Antennas
Ants (Pest Control)
Appliance Repair —
  Major
Appliance Repair — Small

Attics
Awnings

B

Barbecues
Basements and Cellars
Bathrooms
Bedrooms
Beds
Boilers (Heating System)
Bookcases (Shelving)
Box Elder Bugs (Pest
  Control)

Breezeways
Bricklaying
Burglary (Alarm Systems)

C

Cabinets (Storage)
Caning (Furniture —
  Repair)
Carpentry
Carpeting and Rugs
Carports (Garages)
Ceilings

HOMEMAKING

A

Accessories (Decorating or Interior Decorating)
Accidents (Safety)
Activities for Children
Afghans
Alarm Systems
Animals (Pets)
Answering Machine (Telephones)
Antiques
Appliances — Major
Appliances — Small
Appliques
Aprons
Attics
Automobile Care or Car Care

B

Baby Care
Baby Naming
Baby Showers or Showers
Babysitting Tips
Backpacking
Basements
Baskets and Basketweaving
Bathrooms
Batik
Beauty Tips or Make-up
Bedding (Beds and Bedding)
Bedrooms
Beds and Bedding
Bedspreads (Beds and Bedding)
Bicycles and Bicycle Repair
Birdwatching
Birthday Party Ideas
Bookshelves
Budgeting (Money Management)
Bulletin Boards
Burglary (Alarm Systems)

C

Cabinets (Storage)
Camping
Candles

Car Care or Automobile Care
Carpeting and Rugs
Centerpieces
Ceramics
Chairs (Furniture)
Child Development
Children
Children's Rooms
Christmas — Card Ideas and Traditions
Christmas — Decorations
Christmas — Gift Ideas and Gift Wrap
Circus Ideas
Cleaning or Housecleaning
Cleaning Products (Cleaning or Housecleaning)
Closets
Cooperation
Crafts
Crewel
Crocheting
Curtains and Drapes
Cushions or Pillows

D

Dancing
Decorating or Interior Decorating
Decoupage
Dens
Dental Care
Diseases (Medical Facts)
Dividers or Room Dividers
Dog Training
Dolls and Dollhouses
Drapes and Curtains
Dried Flowers
Driftwood Projects

E

Ecology
Egg Decorating
Embroidery
Emergencies
Energy Conservation
Entertaining

Estate Planning
Etiquette or Manners
Exercising
Eye Care

F

Fabric Flowers
Family Cooperation or Cooperation
Family Council
Family Rooms
Father's Day Ideas
Filing (Organization)
Finances (Money Management)
Fire Prevention and Drill
Fireplaces
First Aid
Flower Arranging
Foilcraft
Folding Screens (Dividers or Room Dividers)
Frames and Framing
Furniture

G

Games
Garage Sales
Garages
Gardening
Glass
Gloves (Handwear)
Growth Charts

H

Haircutting and Hair Care
Halloween Ideas
Handiwork
Handwear
Hats
Health
Home Organization or Organization
Home Repairs or Repairs
House — Buying and Selling
Housecleaning or Cleaning
Houseplants or Indoor Plants

CHILD DEVELOPMENT

A

Ability (Talent)
Accident Prevention
(Safety)
Accountability
Acne
Activities
Adolescence
Adoption
Aggressiveness
(Personality)
Allergies
Allowance (Money)
Anger
Animals (Pets)
Anxiety (Fears)
Appetite (Eating Habits)
Art Projects
Attention
Authority
Automobiles (Driving)

B

Babies (Infancy)
Baby Food (Eating Habits)
Baby Talk (Speech)
Babysitter's Tips
Babysitting Cooperatives
Bad Language
(Communication)
Bar Mitzvah
Bathroom Technique
(Toilet Training)
Bedrooms
Bedwetting (Toilet
Training)
Behavior
Birth Defects
Birthday Parties
Biting (Anger)
Bladder Training (Toilet
Training)
Bleeding
Books (Reading)
Bottlefeeding (Eating
Habits)
Braces (Dental Care)
Breastfeeding (Nursing or
Eating Habits)
Bribery (Rewards)

Bronchitis (Illnesses)
Brother-Sister
Relationships (Siblings)
Brushing Teeth (Dental
Care)

C

Candy (Eating Habits)
Camps/Camping
Carelessness
(Responsibility)
Cars (Driving)
Character
Cheating (Honesty)
Chickenpox (Diseases)
Childbirth
Christmas
Circus Ideas
Cleanliness (Grooming)
Clubs
Clumsiness (Motor
Control)
Colds (Illnesses)
Colic (Illnesses)
Colors, Teaching
Communication
Competition
Constipation (Illnesses)
Consumer Awareness,
Teaching
Convulsions (Illnesses)
Cooking, Teaching
Cooperation
Coordination (Motor
Control)
Courage
Creativity (Imagination)
Crushes (Adolescence)
Crying
Curiosity

D

Dating
Day Care Centers
Death, Teaching
Decorating Bedrooms
(Bedrooms)
Dental Care
Depression

Diabetes (Diseases)
Diapers
Diarrhea (Illnesses)
Diet (Eating Habits)
Dieting (Weight Control)
Diptheria (Diseases)
Disabilities
Discipline
Diseases
Divorce
Dolls and Dollhouses
Dramatic Play
Dressing Self
(Independence)
Driving
Drugs

E

Ear Infections (Illnesses)
Ears
Easter Ideas
Eating Habits
Emotions or Feelings
Equality
Etiquette or Manners
Exceptional Children or
Gifted Children
Exercise
Extended Family
Eye Care

F

Failure
Family Cooperation
(Cooperation)
Family Council
Fantasy (Imagination)
Father's Day Ideas
Father's Role
Fears
Feeding (Eating Habits)
Feelings or Emotions
Fever (Illnesses)
Fighting or Quarreling
Fine Motor Control
(Motor Control)
Fingerplays
First Aid
Five-Year Olds
(Preschoolers)

R continued

Rooms (Bedrooms)
Rosh Hashanah
Routine
Rudeness (Respect)
Rules
Running Away (Security)

S

Safety
Sandboxes (Play Yard)
Santa Claus (Christmas)
Sassing (Communication
  or Respect)
Scarlet Fever (Diseases)
School
Scouting
Security
Self-control
Self-image or Self-worth
Sex Education
Shapes — Teaching
Sharing
Shyness
Siblings
Sicknesses (Illnesses)
Sister-Brother
  Relationships (Siblings)
Sleeping Habits
Smallpox (Diseases)
Snacks (Eating Habits)
Songs (Music)
Spanking (Discipline)
Speech
Sports
Stealing (Honesty)

Step-children
Storytelling (Reading)
Study Habits
Stuttering (Speech)
Sugar (Eating Habits)
Swimming

T

Table Manners (Etiquette
  or Manners)
Talents (Ability)
Talking, Learning (Speech)
Tattling
Tears (Crying)
Teasing
Teenagers (Adolescence)
Teeth (Dental Care)
Teething (Dental Care)
Telephone
Television
Temper Tantrums (Anger)
Temperament (Personality)
Tension
Thanksgiving Ideas
Threats (Discipline)
Three-Year Olds (Toddlers)
Thumbsucking
Time, Teaching
Toddlers — Age 2-3
Toilet Training
Tonsilitis (Illnesses)
Touching
  (Communication)
Toys
Traditions
Traveling with Children
Treehouses (Play Yard)

Triplets (Multiple Births)
Twins (Multiple Births)
Two-Year Olds (Toddlers)

U

Untidiness (Organization)

V

Vacations
Vaccinations
  (Immunizations)
Valentine's Day Ideas
Virus (Illnesses)
Vision (Eye Care)
Vitamins (Eating Habits)
Vocational Guidance

W

Walking, Learning
Warts (Illnesses)
Weaning (Eating Habits)
Weeping (Crying)
Weight Control
Whining (Communication)
Whooping Cough
  (Diseases)
Work, Teaching
Worry (Fears)

Y

Yard Equipment (Play
  Yard)
Yelling (Communication)
Yom Kippur

RELIGION

A

Ability or Talent
Abomination
Abstinence or Fasting
Accomplishment or
  Achievement; Success
Accountability or
  Stewardship
Achievement or
  Accomplishment; Success
Actions or Deeds

Adolescence
Adoption
Adultery
Adversity or Opposition
Advice or Counsel
Affection (Kindness or Love)
Affliction or Suffering
Age and Aging
Alcohol
Ambition (Work)
America
Ancestors (Genealogy)

Angels
Anger or Wrath
Animals
Anxiety or Worry
Apathy
Appreciation or Gratitude;
  Thanksgiving
Arguing or Quarreling;
  Fighting
Atonement
Attitude
Authority or Power

B

Backbiting or Gossip
Baptism
Beatitudes
Beauty
Belief
Benevolence or Charity
Bereavement (Death)
Bible
Birth
Blame (Accountability)
Blessings
Bliss (Happiness)
Boasting (Pride)
Bravery (Courage)
Brevity
Brotherhood

C

Challenges
Character
Charity or Benevolence
Chastity
Cheating (Dishonesty)
Children
Christ (Jesus Christ)
Commitment
Communication
Compassion or Mercy
Complaining
Compromise
Conceit (Pride)
Confidence
Confirmation
Conflict (Adversity)
Conscience
Consequences
Contention
Counsel or Advice
Courage (Bravery)
Covenants or Promises;
  Oaths
Creation
Creativity
Criticism

D

Darkness
Dating
Death
Debt (Money)

Deceit (Dishonesty)
Dedication (Enthusiasm)
Deeds or Actions
Delegation
Dependability (Reliance)
Despair
Devil or Satan
Diligence or Effort
Discipline
Discouragement (Despair)
Dishonesty
Divorce

E

Earth
Easter
Eastern Religions
Education
Effort or Diligence
Egoism or Selfishness
Emotions or Feelings
Endurance or
  Perseverence; Persistence
Enemies
Enjoyment (Happiness)
Enthusiasm
Envy or Jealousy
Equality or Justice
Esteem or Respect
Eternal Life
Ethics or Morals
Etiquette or Manners
Evil or Wickedness
Example
Excuses (Apathy)
Experience

F

Failure
Faith
Fame
Family Life
Fasting or Abstinence
Fatherhood
Fearfulness
Feelings or Emotions
Fighting or Quarreling;
  Arguing
Finances (Money)
Forgiveness
Free Agency
Freedom or Liberty

Fretting (Anxiety or
  Worry)
Friendship

G

Gambling
Genealogy
Generosity (Charity)
Goals or Objectives
God
Godhead
Golden Rule
Goodness or Righteousness
Gospel
Gossip or Backbiting
Gratitude or Appreciation;
  Thanksgiving
Greed (Selfishness)
Grief (Despair)
Guidance (Counsel or
  Advice)
Guilt

H

Habits
Hannukah
Happiness or Joy
Hardship
Harmony or Peace
Health
Heaven
Hell
Holy Ghost
Honesty or Integrity
Honor
Human Relations
Humility
Humor
Husband (Marriage)
Hypocrisy (Dishonesty)

I

Ideals
Idleness or Laziness
Ignorance (Knowledge)
Immortality
Improvement
Industry (Work)
Influence
Initiative (Enthusiasm)

I continued

Inspiration
Integrity or Honesty
Intelligence (Knowledge)

J

Jealousy or Envy
Jesus Christ
Joy or Happiness
Judging or Prejudice
Justice or Equality

K

Kindness
Knowledge (Intelligence)

L

Labor (Work)
Laughter (Happiness)
Law
Laziness or Idleness
Leadership
Learning (Education)
Leisure
Liberty or Freedom
Life
Light
Listening (Communication)
Loneliness
Lord (Jesus Christ)
Love
Loyalty
Lying (Dishonesty)

M

Manhood
Manners or Etiquette
Marriage
Meditation
Meekness (Humility)
Mercy or Compassion
Mind (Intelligence)
Miracles
Moderation (Self-Control)
Modesty (Chastity)
Money
Morality (Chastity)
Morals or Ethics
Mortality

Motherhood
Motivation (Attitude)
Mourning (Death)
Music

N

Name
Nature
Neglect (Apathy)
Neighboring
New Testament
New Year

O

Oaths or Promises;
  Covenants
Obedience
Objective or Goal
Obscenity (Profanity)
Offering (Sacrifice)
Old Testament
Opportunity
Opposition or Adversity
Optimism
Order
Organizing

P

Pain (Suffering)
Parables
Pardon (Forgiveness)
Parenthood
Passover
Patience or Tolerance
Patriotism
Peace or Harmony
Perfection
Persecution
Perseverance or
  Endurance; Persistence
Personality
Pessimism
Pioneers
Pity (Compassion or
  Mercy)
Pleasure (Happiness)
Politics
Power or Authority
Praise (Honor)
Prayer
Prejudice or Judging

Preparedness or Readiness
Pride
Procrastination (Apathy)
Profanity (Obscenity)
Progress
Promises or Covenants;
  Oaths
Prophets
Prosperity
Prudence (Modesty)
Punishment
  (Consequences)
Purity (Chastity)

Q

Quarreling or Arguing;
  Fighting
Quietness (Peace)
Quitting

R

Readiness or Preparedness
Redeemer (Jesus Christ)
Reliance (Dependability)
Reputation
Resolutions
Respect or Esteem
Responsibility
Rest
Revenge (Justice)
Reverence
Rewards (Consequences)
Righteousness or Goodness
Rights
Rosh Hashanah

S

Sabbath
Sacrament
Sacrifice (Offerings)
Sadness (Despair)
Salvation
Satan or Devil
Savior (Jesus Christ)
Scriptures
Second Coming
Self-confidence
Self-control
Self-improvement
  (Perfection)

S continued

Selfishness or Egoism
Service
Shame (Guilt)
Sharing (Charity)
Sin or Transgression
Sincerity (Honesty)
Sorrow (Despair)
Speech (Communication)
Spirituality
Sportsmanship
Standards
Steadfastness (Endurance
 or Perseverence;
 Persistence)
Stealing (Dishonesty)
Stewardship or
 Accountability
Strength (Courage)
Success or Achievement;
 Accomplishment
Suffering or Affliction
Swearing (Profanity)
Sympathy (Compassion)

T

Talent or Ability
Teaching and Teachers
 (Education)

Temperance
Temptation
Ten Commandments
Testimony
Tests (Trials)
Thankfulness
 (Appreciation)
Thanksgiving or
 Appreciation; Gratitude
Thrift
Time
Tithing
Tolerance or Patience
Transgression or Sin
Trials
Tribulations
Trust
Truth

U

Understanding
Unity
Universe

V

Valience
Values
Vanity (Pride)

Violence
Virtue

W

War
Weaknesses
Wealth
Welfare
Wickedness or Evil
Willingness
Wisdom (Knowledge)
Wit
Wife (Marriage)
Womanhood
Work or Labor
Worldliness
Worry or Anxiety
Worth
Wrath or Anger

Y

Yom Kippur
Youth

Z

Zeal (Enthusiasm)

SEWING & NEEDLEWORK

A

A-Line
Accessories
Adhesives (Bonding)
Adjustments
Alterations
Appliance Covers
Applique
Aprons
Armholes
Ascots (Scarves)

B

Babywear or Infantwear
Back-wraps (Skirts)
Backpacks (Sleeping Bags)

Bags or Purses
Balmacaan (Coats)
Bargello (Needlepoint)
Bateau/Boat (Necklines)
Bathrobes (Loungewear)
Batik
Beanbag Chair
Bedspreads
Belts and Suspenders
Beveling (Seams)
Bibs
Blankets
Blazers (Jackets)
Blouses
Boleros (Jackets)
Bonding
Bonnets (Hats)
Boutonniere (Buttonholes)

Bows (Decorations)
Boyswear
Braid Trimmings
 (Decorations)
Bras (Lingerie)
Bridalwear or Wedding
 Apparel
Broomstick Lace
 (Crocheting)
Buttonholes

C

Caftans (Loungewear)
Candlewicking
Capes
Caps (Hats)
Cardigans (Sweaters)

P continued

Puritan (Collars)
Purses or Bags

Q

Quilting

R

Raglan (Sleeves)
Rickrack (Decorations)
Robes (Loungewear)
Roman Shades (Curtains)
Ruffles

S

Sashes (Belts and
  Suspenders)
Scarves
Seams
Sewing Machines
Sewing Machines
  —Accessories
Sewing Projects for
  Children
Shawls (Capes)
Sheets
Shifts (Dresses)
Shirts
Shorts
Skirts

Slacks
Sleeping Bags
Sleepwear (Loungewear)
Sleeves
Slipcovers
Slips (Lingerie)
Smocking (Embroidery)
Snaps (Closures)
Soutache (Decorations)
Sportswear
Stitches
Stoles (Capes)
Stripes
Stuffed Toys
Suits
Sundresses
Sunsuits
Suspenders (Belts and
  Suspenders)
Swatches (Fabric Types)
Sweaters
Swimwear

T

T-Shirts
Tablecloths and Runners
Tailoring
Tapestry
Tatting
Ties or Neckties; Cravats
Toddlerwear
Tops
Totebags (Bags)

Trimmings (Decorations)
Turtlenecks (Necklines)

U

Underwear (Lingerie)
Uniforms

V

V-Neck (Necklines)
Valances (Curtains)
Vests (Jackets)
Velcro (Closures)

W

Waistbands
Waistlines
Wallhangings
Weaving
Wedding Apparel
Wrap-arounds (Skirts)

Y

Yokes

Z

Żigzag Sewing
Zippers

COMMUNITY INVOLVEMENT

(Example of subject headings for Citizens Committee Against School Closing; SC is prefix)

SC101 - Pupil Enrollment Figures
SC102 - Budgets and Financial Information
SC103 - Legal Actions
SC104 - District and School Bus Route Maps
SC105 - District Information Handouts
SC106 - Citizens Committee Information Handouts
SC107 - School Board Minutes
SC108 - Citizens Committee Meeting Minutes
SC109 - Public Hearing Records
SC110 - Architects' Reports
SC111 - Citizens Committee Fund Raising

INDEX

Will you share your experience with paper with us?

If you've experienced a frustration or success in coping with paper, do let me know about it. If we can use your experience in a future edition to help others, you will receive a free autographed copy of the book.

If you have a specific question about your paperwork, drop me a line and I'll respond.

I'm looking forward to hearing from you!

Pat Dorff

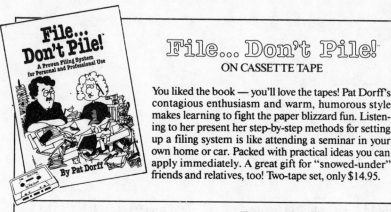

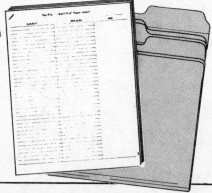

ORDER FORM

Name _____

Address _____

City _____ State _____ Zip _____

Check or money order payable to Willowtree Press. Canadian orders in U.S. funds only. Prepayment required on all orders.

Quant.	Item	Cost Per Item	Amount
	File . . . Don't Pile!™ Cassette Tape	$14.95	
	A-Z Paperdex™	$ 1.95	
	Prefix Paperdex™ Set	$ .95	
	Get Your Feet Wet Filing Kit	$ 7.95	
	Special Combination: Get Your Feet Wet Filing Kit and Cassette Tape Set	$19.95	
	Gift Wrap & Card	$ .50	

PACKING AND DELIVERY COSTS

Orders Totaling	Include
Up to $3.00	$1.50
$3.01 to 6.00	$2.00
$6.01 to 11.00	$2.50
$11.01 to 16.00	$3.00
$16.01 to 23.00	$3.50
$23.01 to 30.00	$4.00
Over $30.00	$4.50

Minn. residents add 6% sales tax	
Shipping & handling	
Total enclosed	

Packages sent to separate addresses require separate postage.
Send to: Willowtree Press, Inc.
Dept. B, 8108-33rd Pl. N.
Minneapolis, MN 55427.

- -

ORDER FORM

Name _____

Address _____

City _____ State _____ Zip _____

Check or money order payable to Willowtree Press. Canadian orders in U.S. funds only. Prepayment required on all orders.

Quant.	Item	Cost Per Item	Amount
	File . . . Don't Pile!™ Cassette Tape	$14.95	
	A-Z Paperdex™	$ 1.95	
	Prefix Paperdex™ Set	$ .95	
	Get Your Feet Wet Filing Kit	$ 7.95	
	Special Combination: Get Your Feet Wet Filing Kit and Cassette Tape Set	$19.95	
	Gift Wrap & Card	$ .50	

PACKING AND DELIVERY COSTS

Orders Totaling	Include
Up to $3.00	$1.50
$3.01 to 6.00	$2.00
$6.01 to 11.00	$2.50
$11.01 to 16.00	$3.00
$16.01 to 23.00	$3.50
$23.01 to 30.00	$4.00
Over $30.00	$4.50

Minn. residents add 6% sales tax	
Shipping & handling	
Total enclosed	

Packages sent to separate addresses require separate postage.
Send to: Willowtree Press, Inc.
Dept. B, 8108-33rd Pl. N.
Minneapolis, MN 55427.

- -

The book. FILE . . . DON'T PILE!™ is available at your local bookstore or may be ordered directly from St. Martin's Press, 175 Fifth Ave., New York, NY 10010.

Pat Dorff, a member of the National Speakers Association, has motivated audiences for over 10 years. Thousands have benefitted from her practical, creative presentations.

For more information write:
Willowtree Press, Inc. Dept. M, 8108-33rd Pl. N., Minneapolis, MN 55427 or call (612) 546-4963.

ORDER FORM

Name _____

Address _____

City _____ State _____ Zip _____

Check or money order payable to Willowtree Press. Canadian orders in U.S. funds only. Prepayment required on all orders.

Quant.	Item	Cost Per Item	Amount
	File . . . Don't Pile!™ Cassette Tape	$14.95	
	A-Z Paperdex™	$ 1.95	
	Prefix Paperdex™ Set	$ .95	
	Get Your Feet Wet Filing Kit	$ 7.95	
	Special Combination: Get Your Feet Wet Filing Kit and Cassette Tape Set	$19.95	
	Gift Wrap & Card	$ .50	

PACKING AND DELIVERY COSTS	
	Minn. residents add 6% sales tax
	Shipping & handling

Orders Totaling	Include
Up to $3.00 ....$1.50	**Total**
$3.01 to 6.00 ....$2.00	**enclosed**
$6.01 to 11.00 ....$2.50	
$11.01 to 16.00 ....$3.00	
$16.01 to 23.00 ....$3.50	
$23.01 to 30.00 ....$4.00	
Over $30.00 ....$4.50	

Packages sent to separate addresses require separate postage.
Send to: Willowtree Press, Inc.
Dept. B, 8108-33rd Pl. N.
Minneapolis, MN 55427.

- -

ORDER FORM

Name _____

Address _____

City _____ State _____ Zip _____

Check or money order payable to Willowtree Press. Canadian orders in U.S. funds only. Prepayment required on all orders.

Quant.	Item	Cost Per Item	Amount
	File . . . Don't Pile!™ Cassette Tape	$14.95	
	A-Z Paperdex™	$ 1.95	
	Prefix Paperdex™ Set	$ .95	
	Get Your Feet Wet Filing Kit	$ 7.95	
	Special Combination: Get Your Feet Wet Filing Kit and Cassette Tape Set	$19.95	
	Gift Wrap & Card	$ .50	

PACKING AND DELIVERY COSTS	
	Minn. residents add 6% sales tax
	Shipping & handling

Orders Totaling	Include
Up to $3.00 ....$1.50	**Total**
$3.01 to 6.00 ....$2.00	**enclosed**
$6.01 to 11.00 ....$2.50	
$11.01 to 16.00 ....$3.00	
$16.01 to 23.00 ....$3.50	
$23.01 to 30.00 ....$4.00	
Over $30.00 ....$4.50	

Packages sent to separate addresses require separate postage.
Send to: Willowtree Press, Inc.
Dept. B, 8108-33rd Pl. N.
Minneapolis, MN 55427.

- -

The book. FILE . . . DON'T PILE!™ is available at your local bookstore or may be ordered directly from St. Martin's Press, 175 Fifth Ave., New York, NY 10010.

Pat Dorff, a member of the National Speakers Association, has motivated audiences for over 10 years. Thousands have benefitted from her practical, creative presentations.

For more information write:
Willowtree Press, Inc. Dept. M, 8108-33rd Pl. N., Minneapolis, MN 55427 or call (612) 546-4963.

ORDER FORM

Name _____

Address _____

City _____ State _____ Zip _____

Check or money order payable to Willowtree Press. Canadian orders in U.S. funds only. Prepayment required on all orders.

Quant.	Item	Cost Per Item	Amount
	File . . . Don't Pile!™ Cassette Tape	$14.95	
	A-Z Paperdex™	$ 1.95	
	Prefix Paperdex™ Set	$ .95	
	Get Your Feet Wet Filing Kit	$ 7.95	
	Special Combination: Get Your Feet Wet Filing Kit and Cassette Tape Set	$19.95	
	Gift Wrap & Card	$ .50	

PACKING AND DELIVERY COSTS

Orders Totaling	Include
Up to $3.00	$1.50
$3.01 to 6.00	$2.00
$6.01 to 11.00	$2.50
$11.01 to 16.00	$3.00
$16.01 to 23.00	$3.50
$23.01 to 30.00	$4.00
Over $30.00	$4.50

Minn. residents add 6% sales tax	
Shipping & handling	
Total enclosed	

Packages sent to separate addresses require separate postage.
Send to: Willowtree Press, Inc.
Dept. B, 8108-33rd Pl. N.
Minneapolis, MN 55427.

- -

ORDER FORM

Name _____

Address _____

City _____ State _____ Zip _____

Check or money order payable to Willowtree Press. Canadian orders in U.S. funds only. Prepayment required on all orders.

Quant.	Item	Cost Per Item	Amount
	File . . . Don't Pile!™ Cassette Tape	$14.95	
	A-Z Paperdex™	$ 1.95	
	Prefix Paperdex™ Set	$ .95	
	Get Your Feet Wet Filing Kit	$ 7.95	
	Special Combination: Get Your Feet Wet Filing Kit and Cassette Tape Set	$19.95	
	Gift Wrap & Card	$ .50	

PACKING AND DELIVERY COSTS

Orders Totaling	Include
Up to $3.00	$1.50
$3.01 to 6.00	$2.00
$6.01 to 11.00	$2.50
$11.01 to 16.00	$3.00
$16.01 to 23.00	$3.50
$23.01 to 30.00	$4.00
Over $30.00	$4.50

Minn. residents add 6% sales tax	
Shipping & handling	
Total enclosed	

Packages sent to separate addresses require separate postage.
Send to: Willowtree Press, Inc.
Dept. B, 8108-33rd Pl. N.
Minneapolis, MN 55427.

- -

The book. FILE . . . DON'T PILE!™ is available at your local bookstore or may be ordered directly from St. Martin's Press, 175 Fifth Ave., New York, NY 10010.

Pat Dorff, a member of the National Speakers Association, has motivated audiences for over 10 years. Thousands have benefitted from her practical, creative presentations.

For more information write:
Willowtree Press, Inc. Dept. M, 8108-33rd Pl. N., Minneapolis, MN 55427 or call (612) 546-4963.